BEST-LOVED
HERSHEY'S®
RECIPES

Publications International, Ltd.

Favorite Brand Name Recipes at www.fbnr.com

Louis Weber, CEO
Publications International, Ltd.
7373 North Cicero Avenue
Lincolnwood, IL 60712

Permission is never granted for commercial purposes.

HERSHEY'S, KISSES, MINI KISSES, MAUNA LOA, HEATH, REESE'S AND SPECIAL DARK are registered trademarks of The Hershey Company, Hershey, PA, 17033. MOUNDS trademark used under license.

Pictured on the front cover: Mocha Cheesecake *(page 24)*.
Pictured on the back cover *(left to right):* Easy Chocolate Cheese Pie *(page 196)*, REESE'S® Peanut Butter and Milk Chocolate Chip Brownies *(page 122)* and Holiday Double Peanut Butter Fudge Cookies *(page 138)*.

ISBN-13: 978-1-4127-2431-9
ISBN-10: 1-4127-2431-7

Library of Congress Control Number: 2006901039

Manufactured in China.

8 7 6 5 4 3 2 1

Microwave Cooking: Microwave ovens vary in wattage. Use the cooking times as guidelines and check for doneness before adding more time.

Preparation/Cooking Times: Preparation times are based on the approximate amount of time required to assemble the recipe before cooking, baking, chilling or serving. These times include preparation steps such as measuring, chopping and mixing. The fact that some preparations and cooking can be done simultaneously is taken into account. Preparation of optional ingredients and serving suggestions is not included.

BEST-LOVED
HERSHEY'S
RECIPES

1

CAKES & CHEESECAKES

HERSHEY'S BEST LOVED CHOCOLATE CHEESECAKE

Quick Chocolate Crumb Crust (recipe follows)
3 packages (8 ounces *each*) cream cheese, softened
1¼ cups sugar
1 container (8 ounces) dairy sour cream
2 teaspoons vanilla extract
½ cup HERSHEY'S Cocoa
2 tablespoons all-purpose flour
3 eggs
Quick Chocolate Drizzle (recipe follows)

1. Prepare Quick Chocolate Crumb Crust. Heat oven to 450°F.

2. Beat cream cheese and sugar until blended. Add sour cream and vanilla; beat until blended. Beat in cocoa and flour. Add eggs, one at a time; beat just until blended. Pour into crust.

3. Bake 10 minutes. *Reduce oven temperature to 250°F;* continue baking 40 minutes. Remove from oven to wire rack. With knife, loosen cake from side of pan. Cool completely; remove side of pan. Prepare Quick Chocolate Drizzle; drizzle over top. Refrigerate 4 to 6 hours. Store covered in refrigerator. *Makes 12 servings*

QUICK CHOCOLATE CRUMB CRUST: Combine 1 cup chocolate wafer crumbs and ¼ cup (½ stick) butter or margarine; press onto bottom of 9-inch springform pan. Makes 1 (9-inch) crust.

QUICK CHOCOLATE DRIZZLE: Place ½ cup HERSHEY'S Semi-Sweet Chocolate Chips and 2 teaspoons shortening (do *not* use butter, margarine, spread or oil) in small microwave-safe bowl. Microwave at HIGH (100%) 30 seconds. If necessary, microwave at HIGH an additional 15 seconds at a time, stirring after each heating, just until chips are melted.

HERSHEY'S BEST LOVED CHOCOLATE CHEESECAKE

TOFFEE-TOPPED PINEAPPLE UPSIDE-DOWN CAKES

$\frac{1}{4}$ cup light corn syrup

$\frac{1}{4}$ cup ($\frac{1}{2}$ stick) butter or margarine, melted

1 cup HEATH® BITS 'O BRICKLE® Toffee Bits

4 pineapple rings

4 maraschino cherries

$\frac{1}{4}$ cup ($\frac{1}{2}$ stick) butter or margarine, softened

$\frac{2}{3}$ cup sugar

1 egg

1 tablespoon rum *or* 1 teaspoon rum extract

$1\frac{1}{3}$ cups all-purpose flour

2 teaspoons baking powder

$\frac{2}{3}$ cup milk

1. Heat oven to 350°F. Lightly coat inside of 4 individual 2-cup baking dishes with vegetable oil spray.

2. Stir together 1 tablespoon corn syrup and 1 tablespoon melted butter in each of 4 baking dishes. Sprinkle each with $\frac{1}{4}$ cup toffee. Center pineapple rings on toffee and place cherries in centers.

3. Beat softened butter and sugar in small bowl until blended. Add egg and rum, beating well. Stir together flour and baking powder; add alternately with milk to butter-sugar mixture, beating until smooth. Spoon about $\frac{3}{4}$ cup batter into each prepared dish.

4. Bake 25 to 30 minutes or until wooden pick inserted in centers comes out clean. Immediately invert onto serving dish. Refrigerate leftovers.   *Makes four (4-inch) cakes*

TIP

Maraschino cherries are sweet cherries
that are pitted, soaked in sugar syrup,
flavored and dyed a vivid red or green.

TOFFEE-TOPPED PINEAPPLE UPSIDE-DOWN CAKE

TRIPLE LAYER CHEESECAKE

Chocolate Crumb Crust (recipe follows)
3 packages (8 ounces *each*) cream cheese, softened
¾ cup sugar
3 eggs
⅓ cup dairy sour cream
3 tablespoons all-purpose flour
1 teaspoon vanilla extract
¼ teaspoon salt
1 cup HERSHEY'S Butterscotch Chips, melted*
1 cup HERSHEY'S Semi-Sweet Chocolate Chips, melted*
1 cup HERSHEY'S Premier White Chips, melted*
Triple Drizzle (recipe follows, optional)

To melt chips: Place chips in separate medium microwave-safe bowls. Microwave at HIGH (100%) 1 minute; stir. If necessary, microwave at HIGH an additional 15 seconds at a time, stirring after each heating, just until chips are melted when stirred.

1. Heat oven to 350°F. Prepare Chocolate Crumb Crust.

2. Beat cream cheese and sugar, in large bowl on medium speed of mixer, until smooth. Add eggs, sour cream, flour, vanilla and salt; beat until blended. Stir 1⅓ cups batter into melted butterscotch chips until smooth; pour into prepared crust. Stir 1⅓ cups batter into melted chocolate chips until smooth; pour over butterscotch layer. Stir remaining batter into melted white chips until smooth; pour over chocolate layer.

3. Bake 55 to 60 minutes or until almost set in center. Remove from oven to wire rack. With knife, immediately loosen cake from side of pan. Cool completely; remove side of pan. Prepare Triple Drizzle, if desired; drizzle, one flavor at a time, over top of cheesecake. Refrigerate about 3 hours. Cover; refrigerate leftover cheesecake.

Makes 12 to 14 servings

CHOCOLATE CRUMB CRUST: Heat oven to 350°F. Stir together 1½ cups vanilla wafer crumbs (about 45 wafers), ½ cup powdered sugar, and ¼ cup HERSHEY'S Cocoa; stir in ⅓ cup melted butter or margarine. Press mixture onto bottom and 1½ inches up side of 9-inch springform pan. Bake 8 minutes. Cool.

TRIPLE DRIZZLE

1 tablespoon *each* HERSHEY'S Butterscotch Chips, HERSHEY'S Semi-Sweet Chocolate Chips *and* HERSHEY'S Premier White Chips
1½ teaspoons shortening (do *not* use butter, margarine, spread or oil), divided

Place 1 tablespoon HERSHEY'S Butterscotch Chips and ½ teaspoon shortening in small microwave-safe bowl. Microwave at HIGH (100%) 30 to 45 seconds; stir. If necessary, microwave an additional 15 seconds at a time, stirring after each heating, just until chips are melted when stirred. Repeat as above with 1 tablespoon HERSHEY'S Semi-Sweet Chocolate Chips and 1 tablespoon HERSHEY'S Premier White Chips.

CHOCOLATE SPICE CAKE

1¾ cups all-purpose flour
1¼ cups sugar
⅓ cup HERSHEY'S Cocoa
2 teaspoons baking soda
1 teaspoon ground cinnamon
½ teaspoon ground nutmeg
¼ teaspoon ground allspice
⅛ teaspoon salt
1½ cups applesauce
½ cup milk
½ cup (1 stick) butter or margarine, melted
1 teaspoon vanilla extract
1 cup chopped nuts (optional)
½ cup raisins
Vanilla Glaze (recipe follows)

1. Heat oven to 350°F. Grease and flour 13×9×2-inch baking pan.

2. Stir together flour, sugar, cocoa, baking soda, cinnamon, nutmeg, allspice and salt in large bowl. Stir in applesauce, milk, butter and vanilla; beat until well blended. Add nuts, if desired, and raisins. Pour batter into prepared pan.

3. Bake 40 to 45 minutes or until wooden pick inserted in center comes out clean. Cool completely in pan on wire rack. Prepare Vanilla Glaze. Drizzle with glaze.

Makes 12 to 15 servings

VANILLA GLAZE: Combine 1¼ cups powdered sugar, 2 tablespoons softened butter or margarine, 1 to 2 tablespoons hot water or milk and ½ teaspoon vanilla extract in medium bowl; beat with whisk until smooth and of desired consistency. Makes about ¾ cup glaze.

CREAMY CINNAMON CHIPS CHEESECAKE

1½ cups graham cracker crumbs
1 cup plus 2 tablespoons sugar, divided
5 tablespoons butter, melted
2 packages (8 ounces *each*) cream cheese softened
1 teaspoon vanilla extract
3 cartons (8 ounces *each*) dairy sour cream
3 eggs, slightly beaten
1⅔ cups (10-ounce package) HERSHEY'S Cinnamon Chips, divided
1 teaspoon shortening (do *not* use butter, margarine, spread or oil)

1. Heat oven to 325°F. Combine graham cracker crumbs, 2 tablespoons sugar and melted butter in medium bowl. Press crumb mixture evenly onto bottom and about 1½ inches up side of 9-inch springform pan. Bake 8 minutes. Remove from oven.

2. Increase oven temperature to 350°F. Beat cream cheese, remaining 1 cup sugar and vanilla on medium speed of mixer until well blended. Add sour cream; beat on low speed until blended. Add eggs; beat on low speed just until blended. Do not overbeat.

3. Pour half of filling into prepared crust. Sprinkle 1⅓ cups chips evenly over filling in pan. Carefully spoon remaining filling over chips. Place on shallow baking pan.

4. Bake about 1 hour or until center is almost set. Remove from oven; cool 10 minutes on wire rack. Using knife or narrow metal spatula, loosen cheesecake from side of pan. Cool on wire rack 30 minutes more. Remove side of pan; cool 1 hour.

5. Combine shortening and remaining ⅓ cup chips in small microwave-safe bowl. Microwave at HIGH (100%) 30 seconds; stir until chips are melted. Drizzle over cheesecake; cover and refrigerate at least 4 hours. Cover and refrigerate leftover cheesecake.

Makes 12 to 14 servings

CREAMY CINNAMON CHIPS CHEESECAKE

CHOCOLATE GLAZED CITRUS POPPY SEED CAKE

1 package (about 18 ounces) lemon cake mix
3 eggs
$\frac{1}{3}$ cup poppy seed
$\frac{1}{3}$ cup milk
1 container (8 ounces) plain lowfat yogurt
1 teaspoon freshly grated lemon peel
Chocolate Citrus Glaze (recipe follows)

1. Heat oven to 350°F. Grease and flour 12-cup fluted tube pan or 10-inch tube pan.

2. Combine cake mix, eggs, poppy seed, milk, yogurt and lemon peel in large bowl; beat until well blended. Pour batter into prepared pan.

3. Bake 40 to 45 minutes or until wooden pick inserted in center comes out clean. Cool 20 minutes; remove from pan to wire rack. Cool completely.

4. Prepare Chocolate Citrus Glaze; spoon over cake, allowing glaze to run down sides.

Makes 12 servings

CHOCOLATE CITRUS GLAZE

2 tablespoons butter or margarine
2 tablespoons HERSHEY'S Cocoa or HERSHEY'S SPECIAL DARK® Cocoa
2 tablespoons water
1 tablespoon orange-flavored liqueur (optional)
$\frac{1}{2}$ teaspoon orange extract
$1\frac{1}{4}$ to $1\frac{1}{2}$ cups powdered sugar

Melt butter in small saucepan over medium heat; remove from heat. Stir in cocoa, water, liqueur, if desired, and orange extract. Whisk in $1\frac{1}{4}$ cups powdered sugar until smooth. If glaze is too thin, whisk in remaining $\frac{1}{4}$ cup powdered sugar. Use immediately.

Makes about $\frac{3}{4}$ cup glaze

CHOCOLATE GLAZED CITRUS POPPY SEED CAKE

MONOGRAMMED MINI CHOCOLATE CAKES

$\frac{1}{2}$ cup (1 stick) butter or margarine
$\frac{1}{2}$ cup water
3 tablespoons HERSHEY'S Cocoa
1 cup all-purpose flour
1 cup sugar
$\frac{1}{2}$ teaspoon baking soda
$\frac{1}{4}$ teaspoon salt
1 egg
$\frac{1}{3}$ cup dairy sour cream
Cocoa Glaze (recipe follows)
Decorating icing in tube, desired color

1. Heat oven to 350°F. Line bottom of 13×9×2-inch baking pan with parchment or wax paper.

2. Combine butter, water and cocoa in small saucepan. Cook over medium heat, stirring constantly, until mixture boils; remove from heat. Stir together flour, sugar, baking soda and salt in medium bowl. Stir in hot cocoa mixture. Add egg and sour cream; beat on medium speed of mixer until well blended. Pour batter into prepared pan.

3. Bake 20 to 22 minutes or until wooden pick inserted in center comes out clean. Cool 10 minutes. Remove from pan to wire rack; carefully remove parchment paper. Cool completely.

4. Cut cake into small pieces, each about 2×1$\frac{3}{4}$ inches. (Cake will be easier to cut if frozen for several hours or up to several days.) Place on wire cooling rack. Prepare Cocoa Glaze; spoon over top of each piece of cake, allowing glaze to run down sides. Allow glaze to set. Garnish with monogram, using decorating icing. Place in foil cup, if desired.

Makes about 24 mini cakes

COCOA GLAZE: Bring $\frac{1}{2}$ cup water and $\frac{1}{4}$ cup ($\frac{1}{2}$ stick) butter to boil in small saucepan. Stir in $\frac{1}{2}$ cup HERSHEY'S Cocoa. Remove from heat; cool slightly. Gradually add 3 cups powdered sugar, stirring with whisk until smooth. Stir in 2 teaspoons vanilla extract. Makes about 1$\frac{1}{2}$ cups glaze.

MONOGRAMMED MINI CHOCOLATE CAKES

HERSHEY'S SPECIAL DARK® TRUFFLE BROWNIE CHEESECAKE

BROWNIE LAYER

6 tablespoons melted butter or margarine

1¼ cups sugar

1 teaspoon vanilla extract

2 eggs

1 cup plus 2 tablespoons all-purpose flour

⅓ cup HERSHEY'S Cocoa

½ teaspoon baking powder

½ teaspoon salt

TRUFFLE CHEESECAKE LAYER

3 packages (8 ounces *each*) cream cheese, softened

¾ cup sugar

4 eggs

¼ cup heavy cream

2 teaspoons vanilla extract

¼ teaspoon salt

2 cups (12-ounce package) HERSHEY'S SPECIAL DARK® Chocolate Chips, divided

½ teaspoon shortening (do *not* use butter, margarine, spread or oil)

1. Heat oven to 350°F. Grease 9-inch springform pan.

2. For Brownie Layer, stir together melted butter, 1¼ cups sugar and 1 teaspoon vanilla. Add 2 eggs; stir until blended. Stir in flour, cocoa, baking powder and ½ teaspoon salt; blend well. Spread in prepared pan. Bake 25 to 30 minutes or until brownie layer pulls away from side of pan.

3. Meanwhile for Truffle Cheesecake Layer, beat cream cheese and ¾ cup sugar with electric mixer on medium speed in large bowl until smooth. Gradually beat in 4 eggs, heavy cream, 2 teaspoons vanilla and ¼ teaspoon salt until well blended.

4. Set aside 2 tablespoons chocolate chips. Place remaining chips in large microwave-safe bowl. Microwave on HIGH (100%) 1½ minutes or until chips are melted and smooth when stirred. Gradually blend melted chocolate into cheesecake batter.

5. Remove Brownie Layer from oven and immediately spoon cheesecake mixture over brownie. Return to oven; continue baking 45 to 50 minutes or until center is almost set. Remove from oven to wire rack. With knife, loosen cake from side of pan. Cool to room temperature. Remove side of pan.

continued on page 20

HERSHEY'S SPECIAL DARK* TRUFFLE BROWNIE CHEESECAKE

Hershey's Special Dark® Truffle Brownie Cheesecake, continued

6. Place remaining 2 tablespoons chocolate chips and shortening in small microwave-safe bowl. Microwave on HIGH (100%) 30 seconds or until chips are melted and mixture is smooth when stirred. Drizzle over top of cheesecake. Cover; refrigerate several hours until cold. Garnish as desired. Cover and refrigerate leftover cheesecake.

Makes 10 to 12 servings

EASY CHOCOLATE LAYER CAKE

8 bars (8-ounce package) HERSHEY'S Semi-Sweet Baking Chocolate, broken into pieces
3 cups all-purpose flour
1½ cups sugar
2 teaspoons baking soda
1 teaspoon salt
2 cups water
⅔ cup vegetable oil
2 tablespoons white vinegar
2 teaspoons vanilla extract

1. Heat oven to 350°F. Grease and flour two 9-inch round baking pans; line bottoms with wax paper.

2. Place chocolate in small microwave-safe bowl. Microwave at HIGH (100%) 1½ to 2 minutes or until chocolate is melted when stirred; cool slightly.

3. Stir together flour, sugar, baking soda and salt in large bowl. Add melted chocolate, water, oil, vinegar and vanilla; beat on medium speed of mixer until well blended. Pour into prepared pans.

4. Bake 30 to 35 minutes or until wooden pick inserted in centers comes out clean. Cool 10 minutes; remove from pans to wire racks. Cool completely. Frost as desired.

Makes 10 to 12 servings

CHOCOLATE CHIP COOKIE DOUGH CHEESEPIE

Cookie Dough (recipe follows)
2 packages (3 ounces *each*) cream cheese, softened
⅓ cup sugar
⅓ cup dairy sour cream
1 egg
½ teaspoon vanilla extract
1 packaged chocolate crumb crust (6 ounces)

1. Prepare Cookie Dough.

2. Heat oven to 350°F.

3. Beat cream cheese and sugar in small bowl on medium speed of mixer until smooth; blend in sour cream, egg and vanilla. Pour into crust. Drop cookie dough by teaspoons evenly onto cream cheese mixture.

4. Bake 35 to 40 minutes or just until almost set in center. Cool completely on wire rack. Cover; refrigerate leftover pie.   *Makes 8 servings*

COOKIE DOUGH

2 tablespoons butter or margarine, softened
¼ cup packed light brown sugar
¼ cup all-purpose flour
1 tablespoon water
¼ teaspoon vanilla extract
1 cup HERSHEY'S Semi-Sweet Chocolate Chips

Beat butter and brown sugar in small bowl until fluffy. Add flour, water and vanilla; beat until blended. Stir in chocolate chips.

CHOCOLATE SQUARES WITH NUTTY CARAMEL SAUCE

1 cup sugar
¾ cup all-purpose flour
½ cup HERSHEY'S SPECIAL DARK® Cocoa or HERSHEY'S Cocoa
½ teaspoon baking powder
½ teaspoon salt
¾ cup vegetable oil
3 eggs
¼ cup milk
½ teaspoon vanilla extract
1 bag (14 ounces) caramel candies
½ cup water
1 cup pecan pieces
Sweetened whipped cream (optional)

1. Heat oven to 350°F. Grease bottom only of 8-inch square baking pan.

2. Stir together sugar, flour, cocoa, baking powder and salt in medium bowl. Add oil, eggs, milk and vanilla; beat until smooth. Pour batter into prepared pan.

3. Bake 35 to 40 minutes or until wooden pick inserted in center comes out clean. Cool completely in pan on wire rack.

4. Remove wrappers from caramels. Combine caramels and water in small saucepan. Cook over low heat, stirring occasionally, until smooth and well blended. Stir in pecans; cool until thickened slightly. Cut cake into squares; serve with warm caramel nut sauce and sweetened whipped cream, if desired. *Makes 9 servings*

TIP

Be sure to use the pan sizes specified in cake recipes. If the pan is too large, the cake will bake too quickly resulting in an overcooked bottom, pale top and coarse texture. If the pan is too small, the cake may spill over in the oven, causing not only a mess but a sunken middle as well.

CHOCOLATE SQUARE WITH NUTTY CARAMEL SAUCE

CHEESECAKE 5 WAYS

Crumb Crust (recipe follows)
3 packages (8 ounces *each*) cream cheese, softened
$3/4$ cup sugar
3 eggs
1 teaspoon vanilla extract

1. Prepare Crumb Crust. Heat oven to 350°F.

2. Beat cream cheese and sugar in large bowl until smooth. Add eggs, one at a time, beating well after each addition. Stir in vanilla. Pour into prepared crust.

3. Bake 45 to 50 minutes or until almost set.* Remove from oven to wire rack. With knife, loosen cake from side of pan. Cool completely; remove side of pan.

4. Cover; refrigerate several hours or until chilled. Just before serving, garnish as desired. Cover and refrigerate leftover cheesecake. *Makes 10 to 12 servings*

Cheesecakes are less likely to crack if baked in a water bath.

CRUMB CRUST: Heat oven to 350°F. Stir together 1 cup graham cracker crumbs and 2 tablespoons sugar in small bowl; blend in $1/4$ cup ($1/2$ stick) melted butter or margarine, mixing well. Press mixture onto bottom and $1/2$ inch up side of 9-inch springform pan. Bake 8 to 10 minutes. Cool.

CHOCOLATE CHEESECAKE: Increase sugar to $1 1/4$ cups and add $1/3$ cup HERSHEY'S Cocoa. Increase vanilla extract to $1 1/2$ teaspoons.

TOFFEE BITS CHEESECAKE: Prepare cheesecakes as directed. Stir $1 1/3$ cups (8-ounce package) HEATH® BITS 'O BRICKLE® Almond Toffee Bits into batter.

CHOCOLATE CHIP CHEESECAKE: Prepare cheesecake as directed. Stir 1 to $1 1/2$ cups HERSHEY'S MINI CHIPS™ Semi-Sweet Chocolate Chips into batter.

MOCHA CHEESECAKE: Prepare Chocolate Cheesecake, using HERSHEY'S SPECIAL DARK® Cocoa. Add $1 1/2$ teaspoons instant coffee granules to batter.

MOCHA TOFFEE WITH CHOCOLATE CHIPS CHEESECAKE: Prepare Mocha Cheesecake as directed. Stir $3/4$ cup HEATH® BITS 'O BRICKLE® Toffee Bits and $3/4$ cup HERSHEY'S MINI CHIPS™ Semi-Sweet Chocolate Chips into batter.

MOCHA CHEESECAKE

RICH CHOCOLATE MINI-CAKES

$^2/_3$ cup all-purpose flour
$^1/_2$ cup sugar
3 tablespoons HERSHEY'S Cocoa
$^1/_2$ teaspoon baking powder
$^1/_4$ teaspoon baking soda
$^1/_4$ teaspoon salt
$^1/_2$ cup water
3 tablespoons vegetable oil
1 teaspoon vanilla extract
Chocolate Glaze (recipe follows)
Vanilla Drizzle (recipe follows)

1. Heat oven to 350°F. Lightly grease 24 small muffin cups ($1^3/_4$ inches in diameter).

2. Stir together flour, sugar, cocoa, baking powder, baking soda and salt in medium bowl. Add water, oil and vanilla; stir or whisk until batter is smooth and blended. (Batter will be thin.) Spoon batter into prepared cups, filling $^2/_3$ full.

3. Bake 12 to 14 minutes or until top springs back when touched lightly in center. Cool in pans on wire racks 3 minutes; invert onto racks. Cool completely.

4. Prepare Chocolate Glaze; dip rounded portion of cakes into glaze or spread glaze on tops. Place on wax paper-covered tray; refrigerate 10 minutes to set glaze. Prepare Vanilla Drizzle; drizzle onto mini-cakes. Decorate as desired.

Makes about 2 dozen mini-cakes

CHOCOLATE GLAZE: Melt 2 tablespoons butter or margarine in small saucepan over low heat; add 2 tablespoons HERSHEY'S Cocoa and 2 tablespoons water. Cook and stir until smooth and slightly thickened; *do not boil.* Remove from heat; cool slightly. Gradually blend in 1 cup powdered sugar and $^1/_2$ teaspoon vanilla extract; beat with wire whisk until smooth and slightly thickened. Makes about $^1/_2$ cup glaze.

VANILLA DRIZZLE: Place $^1/_2$ cup HERSHEY'S Premier White Chips and 1 tablespoon shortening (do *not* use butter, margarine, spread or oil) in small microwave-safe bowl. Microwave at HIGH (100%) 30 seconds; stir until smooth. If necessary, microwave at HIGH additional 15 seconds or just until chips are melted and smooth when stirred.

RICH CHOCOLATE MINI-CAKES

REESE'S® PEANUT BUTTER AND MILK CHOCOLATE CHIP LAYERED CHEESECAKE

$1\frac{1}{2}$ cups graham cracker crumbs

$\frac{1}{3}$ cup plus 1 cup sugar, divided

$\frac{1}{3}$ cup HERSHEY'S Cocoa

$\frac{1}{4}$ cup ($\frac{1}{2}$ stick) butter, melted

2 packages (8 ounces *each*) cream cheese, softened

1 teaspoon vanilla extract

3 cartons (8 ounces *each*) dairy sour cream

3 eggs, slightly beaten

$1\frac{3}{4}$ cups (11-ounce package) REESE'S® Peanut Butter and Milk Chocolate Chips, divided

1 teaspoon shortening (do *not* use butter, margarine, spread or oil)

1. Heat oven to 325°F. Combine graham cracker crumbs, $\frac{1}{3}$ cup sugar, cocoa and melted butter in medium bowl. Press crumb mixture evenly onto bottom and about $1\frac{1}{2}$ inches up side of 9-inch springform pan. Bake 8 minutes; remove from oven. Cool slightly.

2. *Increase oven temperature to 350°F.* Beat cream cheese, remaining 1 cup sugar and vanilla on medium speed of mixer until well blended. Add sour cream; beat on low speed until blended. Add eggs; beat on low speed just until blended. Do not overbeat.

3. Pour 2 cups filling into prepared crust. Reserve $\frac{1}{4}$ cup chips for drizzle. Sprinkle remaining $1\frac{1}{2}$ cups chips evenly over filling in pan. Carefully spoon remaining filling over chips.

4. Bake about 1 hour or until center is almost set. Remove from oven. Using knife or narrow metal spatula, loosen cheesecake from side of pan. Cool on wire rack additional 30 minutes. Remove side of pan; cool 1 hour.

5. Combine shortening and reserved $\frac{1}{4}$ cup chips in small microwave-safe bowl. Microwave at HIGH (100%) 30 seconds; stir. If necessary, microwave at HIGH an additional 15 seconds at a time, stirring after each heating, until chips are melted and mixture is smooth when stirred. Drizzle over cheesecake; cover and refrigerate at least 4 hours. Cover; refrigerate leftover cheesecake. *Makes 12 to 14 servings*

REESE'S PEANUT BUTTER AND MILK CHOCOLATE CHIP LAYERED CHEESECAKE

HERSHEY'S KISSES® BIRTHDAY CAKE

        2 cups sugar
    1¾ cups all-purpose flour
        ¾ cup HERSHEY'S Cocoa or HERSHEY'S SPECIAL DARK® Cocoa
    1½ teaspoons baking powder
    1½ teaspoons baking soda
        1 teaspoon salt
        2 eggs
        1 cup milk
        ½ cup vegetable oil
        2 teaspoons vanilla extract
        1 cup boiling water
          Vanilla Buttercream Frosting (recipe follows)
          HERSHEY'S KISSES® Brand Milk Chocolates

1. Heat oven to 350°F. Grease and flour two 9-inch round baking pans or one 13×9×2-inch baking pan.

2. Stir together sugar, flour, cocoa, baking powder, baking soda and salt in large bowl. Add eggs, milk, oil and vanilla; beat with electric mixer on medium speed for 2 minutes. Stir in boiling water (batter will be thin). Pour batter into prepared pans.

3. Bake 30 to 35 minutes for round pans, 35 to 40 minutes for rectangular pan or until wooden pick inserted in center comes out clean. Cool 10 minutes; turn out onto wire racks. Cool completely. Prepare Vanilla Buttercream Frosting.

4. Frost with Vanilla Buttercream Frosting. Remove wrappers from chocolates. Garnish top and sides of cake with chocolates. *Makes 10 to 12 servings*

VANILLA BUTTERCREAM FROSTING

    ⅓ cup butter or margarine, softened
    4 cups powdered sugar, divided
    3 to 4 tablespoons milk
    1½ teaspoons vanilla extract

Beat butter with electric mixer on medium speed in large bowl until creamy. With mixer running, gradually add about 2 cups powdered sugar, beating until well blended. Slowly beat in milk and vanilla. Gradually add remaining powdered sugar, beating until smooth. Add additional milk, if necessary, until frosting is desired consistency.

Makes about 2⅓ cups frosting

HERSHEY.'S KISSES® BIRTHDAY CAKE

AUTUMN PEANUTTY CARROT CAKE

3 eggs
¾ cup vegetable oil
1 teaspoon vanilla extract
1½ cups all-purpose flour
¾ cup granulated sugar
½ cup packed light brown sugar
2 teaspoons ground cinnamon
1¼ teaspoons baking soda
2 cups grated carrots
1⅔ cups (10-ounce package) REESE'S® Peanut Butter Chips
½ cup chopped walnuts
Cream Cheese Frosting (recipe follows)

1. Heat oven to 350°F. Grease and flour two 8-inch round baking pans.

2. Beat eggs, oil and vanilla in large bowl. Stir together flour, granulated sugar, brown sugar, cinnamon and baking soda; add to egg mixture and blend well. Stir in carrots, peanut butter chips and walnuts; pour into prepared pans.

3. Bake 30 to 35 minutes or until wooden pick inserted in center comes out clean. Cool 10 minutes; remove from pans to wire rack. Cool completely. Prepare Cream Cheese Frosting. Frost cake.Cover; refrigerate leftover cake.   *Makes 10 to 12 servings*

CREAM CHEESE FROSTING: Beat 2 packages (3 ounces *each*) softened cream cheese and ½ cup (1 stick) softened butter until smooth. Gradually add 4 cups powdered sugar and 2 teaspoons vanilla extract, beating until smooth.

CHOCOLATE AND VANILLA-SWIRLED CHEESE PIE

2 packages (8 ounces *each*) cream cheese, softened
½ cup sugar
1 teaspoon vanilla extract
2 eggs
1 prepared deep-dish crumb crust (9 ounces)
1 cup HERSHEY'S SPECIAL DARK® Chocolate Chips
¼ cup milk
Red raspberry jam (optional)

1. Heat oven to 350°F.

2. Beat cream cheese, sugar and vanilla in mixer bowl until well blended. Add eggs; mix thoroughly. Spread 2 cups batter in crumb crust.

3. Place chocolate chips in medium microwave-safe bowl. Microwave at HIGH (100%) 1 minute; stir. If necessary, microwave an additional 15 seconds at a time, stirring after each heating, until chocolate is melted and smooth when stirred. Cool slightly. Add melted chocolate and milk to remaining batter; blend thoroughly. Drop chocolate batter by tablespoonfuls onto vanilla batter. Gently swirl with knife for marbled effect.

4. Bake 30 to 35 minutes or until center is almost set. Cool; refrigerate several hours or overnight. Drizzle with warmed red raspberry jam, if desired. Cover and refrigerate leftover pie.   *Makes 8 servings*

CHOCOLATE CAKE FINGERS

> 1 cup sugar
> 1 cup all-purpose flour
> $\frac{1}{3}$ cup HERSHEY'S Cocoa
> $\frac{3}{4}$ teaspoon baking powder
> $\frac{3}{4}$ teaspoon baking soda
> $\frac{1}{2}$ cup nonfat milk
> $\frac{1}{4}$ cup frozen egg substitute, thawed
> $\frac{1}{4}$ cup canola oil or vegetable oil
> 1 teaspoon vanilla extract
> $\frac{1}{2}$ cup boiling water
>   Powdered sugar
> 1 teaspoon freshly grated orange peel
> $1\frac{1}{2}$ cups frozen light non-dairy whipped topping, thawed

1. Heat oven to 350°F. Line bottom of 13×9×2-inch baking pan with wax paper.

2. Stir together sugar, flour, cocoa, baking powder and baking soda in large bowl. Add milk, egg substitute, oil and vanilla; beat on medium speed of mixer 2 minutes. Stir in boiling water (batter will be thin). Pour into prepared pan.

3. Bake 16 to 18 minutes or until wooden pick inserted in center comes out clean. With knife or metal spatula, loosen cake from edges of pan. Place clean, lint-free dishtowel on wire rack; sprinkle lightly with powdered sugar. Invert cake on towel; peel off wax paper. Cool completely.

4. Invert cake, right side up, on cutting board. Cut cake into small rectangles (about 2×1$\frac{1}{4}$ inches). Stir orange peel into whipped topping; spoon dollop on each piece of cake. Garnish as desired. Store ungarnished cake, covered, at room temperature.

Makes 42 pieces

STRAWBERRY CHOCOLATE CHIP SHORTCAKE

1 cup sugar, divided

½ cup (1 stick) butter or margarine, softened

1 egg

2 teaspoons vanilla extract, divided

1½ cups all-purpose flour

½ teaspoon baking powder

1 cup HERSHEY'S MINI CHIPS™ Semi-Sweet Chocolate or HERSHEY'S Semi-Sweet Chocolate Chips, divided

1 container (16 ounces) dairy sour cream

2 eggs

2 cups frozen non-dairy whipped topping, thawed

Fresh strawberries, rinsed and halved

1. Heat oven to 350°F. Grease 9-inch springform pan.

2. Beat ½ cup sugar and butter in large bowl. Add 1 egg and 1 teaspoon vanilla; beat until creamy. Gradually add flour and baking powder, beating until smooth; stir in ½ cup small chocolate chips. Press mixture onto bottom of prepared pan.

3. Stir together sour cream, remaining ½ cup sugar, 2 eggs and remaining 1 teaspoon vanilla in medium bowl; stir in remaining ½ cup small chocolate chips. Pour over mixture in pan.

4. Bake 50 to 55 minutes until almost set in center and edges are lightly browned. Cool completely on wire rack; remove side of pan. Spread whipped topping over top. Cover; refrigerate. Just before serving, arrange strawberry halves on top of cake; garnish as desired. Refrigerate leftover dessert. *Makes 12 servings*

TIP

Chocolate should be stored in a cool, dry place (60°F to 70°F.) When chocolate is exposed to varying temperatures, "bloom", a gray-white film, sometimes appears on the surface. It does not affect the taste or quality of the chocolate.

STRAWBERRY CHOCOLATE CHIP SHORTCAKE

FUDGE TRUFFLE CHEESECAKE

Chocolate Crumb Crust (recipe follows)
2 cups (12-ounce package) HERSHEY'S Semi-Sweet Chocolate Chips
3 packages (8 ounces *each*) cream cheese, softened
1 can (14 ounces) sweetened condensed milk (not evaporated milk)
4 eggs
2 teaspoons vanilla extract

1. Prepare Chocolate Crumb Crust; set aside. Heat oven to 300°F.

2. Place chocolate chips in microwave-safe bowl. Microwave at HIGH (100%) 1½ minutes; stir. If necessary, microwave at HIGH an additional 15 seconds at a time, stirring after each heating, just until chips are melted when stirred.

3. Beat cream cheese in large bowl until fluffy. Gradually beat in sweetened condensed milk until smooth. Add melted chips, eggs and vanilla; mix well. Pour into prepared crust.

4. Bake 1 hour and 5 minutes or until center is set. Remove from oven to wire rack. With knife, loosen cake from side of pan. Cool completely; remove side of pan. Refrigerate several hours before serving. Garnish as desired. Cover; refrigerate leftover cheesecake.   *Makes 10 to 12 servings*

CHOCOLATE CRUMB CRUST: Stir together 1½ cups vanilla wafer crumbs, ½ cup powdered sugar, ⅓ cup HERSHEY'S Cocoa and ⅓ cup melted butter or margarine in bowl. Press firmly onto bottom of 9-inch springform pan.

Prep Time: 25 minutes
Bake Time: 1 hour 5 minutes
Cool Time: 1½ hours
Chill Time: 4 hours

FUDGE TRUFFLE CHEESECAKE

HERSHEY'S "PERFECTLY CHOCOLATE" CHOCOLATE CAKE

2 cups sugar

1¾ cups all-purpose flour

¾ cup HERSHEY'S Cocoa or HERSHEY'S Special Dark® Cocoa

1½ teaspoons baking powder

1½ teaspoons baking soda

1 teaspoon salt

2 eggs

1 cup milk

½ cup vegetable oil

2 teaspoons vanilla extract

1 cup boiling water

"Perfectly Chocolate" Chocolate Frosting (recipe follows)

1. Heat oven to 350°F. Grease and flour two 9-inch round baking pans.*

2. Stir together sugar, flour, cocoa, baking powder, baking soda and salt in large bowl. Add eggs, milk, oil and vanilla; beat on medium speed of mixer 2 minutes. Stir in water. (Batter will be thin.) Pour batter evenly into prepared pans.

3. Bake 30 to 35 minutes or until wooden pick inserted in center comes out clean. Cool 10 minutes; remove from pans to wire racks. Cool completely.

4. Prepare "Perfectly Chocolate" Chocolate Frosting; spread between layers and over top and sides of cake. *Makes 8 to 10 servings*

One 13×9×2-inch baking pan may be substituted for 9-inch round baking pans. Prepare as directed above. Bake 35 to 40 minutes. Cool completely in pan on wire rack. Frost as desired.

"PERFECTLY CHOCOLATE" CHOCOLATE FROSTING

½ cup (1 stick) butter or margarine

⅔ cup HERSHEY'S Cocoa

3 cups powdered sugar

⅓ cup milk

1 teaspoon vanilla extract

1. Melt butter. Stir in cocoa. Alternately add powdered sugar and milk, beating to spreading consistency.

2. Add small amount additional milk, if needed. Stir in vanilla.

Makes about 2 cups frosting

HERSHEY'S "PERFECTLY CHOCOLATE" CHOCOLATE CAKE

CAPPUCCINO KISSED CHEESECAKE

1½ cups chocolate cookie crumbs
6 tablespoons butter or margarine, melted
1¼ cups HERSHEY'S MINI KISSES® Brand Milk Chocolates, divided
4 packages (8 ounces *each*) cream cheese, softened
⅔ cup sugar
3 eggs
⅓ cup milk
1 tablespoon instant espresso powder
¼ teaspoon ground cinnamon
Espresso Cream (recipe follows)

1. Heat oven to 350°F. Combine cookie crumbs and butter; press onto bottom and 1 inch up side of 9-inch springform pan.

2. Melt 1 cup chocolate pieces in small saucepan over low heat, stirring constantly. Combine cream cheese and sugar in large bowl, beating on medium speed of mixer until well blended. Add eggs, milk, espresso powder and cinnamon; beat on low speed until well-blended. Add melted chocolate pieces; beat on medium 2 minutes. Spoon mixture into crust.

3. Bake 55 minutes. Remove from oven to wire rack. Cool 15 minutes; with knife, loosen cake from side of pan. Cool completely; remove side of pan. Cover; refrigerate at least 4 hours before serving. Prepare Espresso Cream.

4. To serve, garnish with Espresso Cream and remaining ¼ cup chocolates. Cover; refrigerate leftover cheesecake. *Makes 16 servings*

ESPRESSO CREAM: Beat ½ cup cold whipping cream, 2 tablespoons powdered sugar and 1 teaspoon instant espresso powder until stiff.

CAPPUCCINO KISSED CHEESECAKE

CHOCOLATE CHERRY DELIGHT CAKE

1 cup sugar

1 cup all-purpose flour

$\frac{1}{3}$ cup HERSHEY'S Cocoa

$\frac{3}{4}$ teaspoon baking soda

$\frac{3}{4}$ teaspoon baking powder

Dash salt

$\frac{1}{2}$ cup nonfat milk

$\frac{1}{4}$ cup frozen egg substitute, thawed

$\frac{1}{4}$ cup vegetable oil

1 teaspoon vanilla extract

$\frac{1}{2}$ cup boiling water

Whipped Topping (recipe follows)

1 can (20 ounces) reduced-calorie cherry pie filling, chilled

1. Heat oven to 350°F. Line bottom of two 9-inch round pans with wax paper.

2. Combine sugar, flour, cocoa, baking soda, baking powder and salt in large bowl. Add milk, egg substitute, oil and vanilla; beat on medium speed of mixer 2 minutes. Stir in boiling water. (Batter will be thin.) Pour into prepared pans.

3. Bake 18 to 22 minutes or until wooden pick inserted in centers comes out clean. Cool 10 minutes; remove from pans to wire racks. Carefully remove wax paper. Cool completely.

4. To assemble dessert, place one cake layer on serving plate. Prepare Whipped Topping. Spread with half of topping; top with half of pie filling. Top with second cake layer. Spread with remaining topping and pie filling. Refrigerate at least one hour.

Makes 12 servings

WHIPPED TOPPING: Blend $\frac{1}{2}$ cup cold nonfat milk, $\frac{1}{2}$ teaspoon vanilla extract and 1 envelope (1.3 ounces) dry whipped topping mix in small, deep narrow-bottom bowl. Whip at high speed with mixer until topping peaks, about 2 minutes. Continue beating 2 minutes longer until topping is light and fluffy.

CHOCOLATE CHERRY DELIGHT CAKE

HERSHEY'S RED VELVET CAKE

½ cup (1 stick) butter or margarine, softened
1½ cups sugar
2 eggs
1 teaspoon vanilla extract
1 cup buttermilk or sour milk*
2 tablespoons (1-ounce bottle) red food color
2 cups all-purpose flour
⅓ cup HERSHEY'S Cocoa
1 teaspoon salt
1½ teaspoons baking soda
1 tablespoon white vinegar
1 can (16 ounces) ready-to-spread vanilla frosting
HERSHEY'S MINI CHIPS™ Semi-Sweet Chocolate Chips or HERSHEY'S Milk Chocolate Chips (optional)

To sour milk: Use 1 tablespoon white vinegar plus milk to equal 1 cup.

1. Heat oven to 350°F. Grease and flour 13×9×2-inch baking pan.**

2. Beat butter and sugar in large bowl; add eggs and vanilla, beating well. Stir together buttermilk and food color. Stir together flour, cocoa and salt; add alternately to butter mixture with buttermilk mixture, mixing well. Stir in baking soda and vinegar. Pour into prepared pan.

3. Bake 30 to 35 minutes or until wooden pick inserted in center comes out clean. Cool completely in pan on wire rack. Frost; garnish with chocolate chips, if desired.

Makes about 15 servings

**This recipe can be made in 2 (9-inch) cake pans. Bake at 350°F for 30 to 35 minutes.

HERSHEY'S RED VELVET CAKE

PIES, TARTS, & TORTES

REESE'S® PEANUT BUTTER AND MILK CHOCOLATE CHIP COOKIE PIE

$\frac{1}{2}$ cup (1 stick) butter or margarine, softened

2 eggs, beaten

2 teaspoons vanilla extract

1 cup sugar

$\frac{1}{2}$ cup all-purpose flour

1$\frac{3}{4}$ cups (11-ounce package) REESE'S ® Peanut Butter and Milk Chocolate Chips

1 cup chopped pecans or walnuts

1 unbaked 9-inch pie crust

Sweetened whipped cream or ice cream (optional)

1. Heat oven to 350°F.

2. Beat butter in medium bowl; add eggs and vanilla. Stir together sugar and flour; add to butter mixture. Stir in chips and nuts; pour into unbaked pie crust.

3. Bake 50 to 55 minutes or until golden brown. Cool about 1 hour on wire rack. Serve warm with sweetened whipped cream or ice cream, if desired. To reheat; microwave one slice at a time at HIGH (100%) 10 to 15 seconds. *Makes 8 to 10 servings*

TIP

Pecans can be stored in an airtight container up to 3 months in the refrigerator and up to 6 months in the freezer.

REESE'S* PEANUT BUTTER AND MILK CHOCOLATE CHIP COOKIE PIE

BERRY-BERRY BROWNIE TORTE

½ cup all-purpose flour
¼ teaspoon baking soda
¼ teaspoon salt
1 cup HERSHEY'S Semi-Sweet Chocolate Chips
½ cup (1 stick) butter or margarine
1¼ cups sugar, divided
2 eggs
1 teaspoon vanilla extract
⅓ cup HERSHEY'S SPECIAL DARK® Cocoa
½ cup whipping cream
¾ cup fresh blackberries, rinsed and patted dry
¾ cup fresh raspberries, rinsed and patted dry

1. Heat oven to 350°F. Line 9-inch round baking pan with wax paper, then grease. Stir together flour, baking soda and salt. Stir in chocolate chips.

2. Melt butter in medium saucepan over low heat. Remove from heat. Stir in 1 cup sugar, eggs and vanilla. Add cocoa, blending well. Stir in flour mixture. Spread mixture in prepared pan.

3. Bake 20 to 25 minutes or until wooden pick inserted in center comes out slightly sticky. Cool in pan on wire rack 15 minutes. Invert onto wire rack; remove wax paper. Turn right side up; cool completely.

4. Beat whipping cream and remaining ¼ cup sugar until sugar is dissolved and stiff peaks form. Spread over top of brownie. Top with berries. Refrigerate until serving time.   *Makes 8 to 10 servings*

BERRY-BERRY BROWNIE TORTE

CHOCOLATE STRAWBERRY FRUIT TART

1⅓ cups all-purpose flour
½ cup powdered sugar
¼ cup HERSHEY'S Cocoa or HERSHEY'S SPECIAL DARK® Cocoa
¾ cup (1½ sticks) butter or margarine, softened
Strawberry Vanilla Filling (recipe follows)
½ cup HERSHEY'S Semi-Sweet Chocolate Chips
1 tablespoon shortening (do *not* use butter, margarine, spread or oil)
Glazed Fruit Topping (page 80)
Fresh fruit, sliced

1. Heat oven to 325°F. Grease and flour 12-inch pizza pan.

2. Stir together flour, powdered sugar and cocoa in medium bowl. With pastry blender, cut in butter until mixture holds together; press into prepared pan.

3. Bake 10 to 15 minutes or until crust is set. Cool completely. Prepare Strawberry Vanilla Filling; spread over crust to within 1 inch of edge; refrigerate until filling is firm.

4. Place chocolate chips and shortening in small microwave-safe bowl. Microwave at HIGH (100%) 30 seconds; stir. If necessary, microwave at HIGH an additional 15 seconds at a time, stirring after each heating, just until chips are melted when stirred. Spoon chocolate into disposable pastry bag or corner of heavy duty plastic bag; cut off small piece at corner. Squeeze chocolate onto outer edge of filling in decorative design; refrigerate until chocolate is firm.

5. Prepare Glazed Fruit Topping. Arrange fresh fruit over filling; carefully brush prepared topping over fruit. Refrigerate until ready to serve. Cover; refrigerate leftover tart. *Makes 12 servings*

STRAWBERRY VANILLA FILLING

2 cups (12-ounce package) HERSHEY'S Premier White Chips
¼ cup evaporated milk
1 package (8 ounces) cream cheese, softened
1 teaspoon strawberry extract
2 drops red food color

1. Place white chips and evaporated milk in medium microwave-safe bowl. Microwave at HIGH (100%) 1 minute; stir. If necessary, microwave at HIGH an additional 15 seconds at a time, stirring after each heating, just until chips are melted when stirred.

2. Beat in cream cheese, strawberry extract and red food color.

continued on page 54

CHOCOLATE STRAWBERRY FRUIT TART

Chocolate Strawberry Fruit Tart, continued

GLAZED FRUIT TOPPING

$\frac{1}{4}$ teaspoon unflavored gelatin

1 teaspoon cold water

$\frac{1}{4}$ cup apricot nectar or orange juice

2 tablespoons sugar

$1\frac{1}{2}$ teaspoons cornstarch or arrowroot

$\frac{1}{2}$ teaspoon lemon juice

1. Sprinkle gelatin over water in small cup; let stand 2 minutes to soften.

2. Stir together apricot nectar, sugar, cornstarch and lemon juice in small saucepan. Cook over medium heat, stirring constantly, until mixture is thickened. Remove from heat; immediately stir in gelatin until smooth. Cool slightly.

CHOCOLATE MACAROON HEATH® PIE

$\frac{1}{2}$ cup (1 stick) butter or margarine, melted

3 cups MOUNDS® Sweetened Coconut Flakes

2 tablespoons all-purpose flour

$1\frac{1}{3}$ cups (8-ounce package) HEATH® Milk Chocolate Toffee Bits, divided

$\frac{1}{2}$ gallon chocolate ice cream, softened

1. Heat oven to 375°F.

2. Combine butter, coconut and flour in medium bowl. Press into 9-inch pie pan.

3. Bake 10 minutes or until edge is light golden brown. Cool completely.

4. Set aside $\frac{1}{3}$ cup toffee bits. Combine ice cream and remaining toffee bits. Spread into cooled crust. Sprinkle with $\frac{1}{3}$ cup reserved toffee. Freeze at least 5 hours. Remove from freezer about 10 minutes before serving. *Makes 6 to 8 servings*

FUDGEY PEANUT BUTTER CHIP BROWNIE PIE

    2 eggs
    1 teaspoon vanilla extract
    1 cup sugar
$\frac{1}{2}$ cup (1 stick) butter or margarine, melted
$\frac{1}{2}$ cup all-purpose flour
$\frac{1}{3}$ cup HERSHEY'S Cocoa
$\frac{1}{4}$ teaspoon salt
$\frac{2}{3}$ cup REESE'S® Peanut Butter Chips
    1 packaged butter-flavored crumb crust (6 ounces)
    Peanut Butter Sauce (recipe follows)
    Vanilla ice cream

1. Heat oven to 350°F.

2. Lightly beat eggs and vanilla in medium bowl; blend in sugar and butter. Stir together flour, cocoa and salt. Add to egg mixture; beat until blended. Stir in peanut butter chips. Place crust on baking sheet; pour chocolate mixture into crust.

3. Bake 45 to 50 minutes or until set; cool completely on wire rack. Prepare Peanut Butter Sauce; serve over pie and ice cream. *Makes 8 servings*

PEANUT BUTTER SAUCE

    1 cup REESE'S® Peanut Butter Chips
$\frac{1}{3}$ cup milk
$\frac{1}{4}$ cup whipping cream
$\frac{1}{4}$ teaspoon vanilla extract

Combine peanut butter chips, milk and whipping cream in small saucepan over low heat. Cook, stirring constantly, until chips are melted and mixture is smooth. Remove from heat; stir in vanilla. Serve warm. *Makes 1 cup sauce*

REESE'S® PEANUT BUTTER & HERSHEY'S KISSES® PIE

About 42 HERSHEY'S KISSES® Brand Milk Chocolates, divided
2 tablespoons milk
1 packaged (8-inch) crumb crust (6 ounces)
1 package (8 ounces) cream cheese, softened
¾ cup sugar
1 cup REESE'S® Creamy or Crunchy Peanut Butter
1 tub (8 ounces) frozen non-dairy whipped topping, thawed and divided

1. Remove wrappers from chocolates. Place 26 chocolates and milk in small microwave-safe bowl. Microwave on HIGH (100%) 1 minute or just until melted and smooth when stirred. Spread evenly on bottom of crust. Refrigerate about 30 minutes.

2. Beat cream cheese with electric mixer on medium speed in medium bowl until smooth; gradually beat in sugar, then peanut butter, beating well after each addition. Reserve ½ cup whipped topping; fold remaining whipped topping into peanut butter mixture. Spoon into crust over chocolate. Cover; refrigerate about 6 hours or until set.

3. Garnish with reserved whipped topping and remaining chocolates. Cover; refrigerate leftover pie.

Makes 8 servings

TIP

To soften cream cheese quickly,
remove it from the wrapper and place it on
a medium microwavable plate. Microwave
on MEDIUM (50%) 15 to 20 seconds
or until slightly softened.

REESE'S° PEANUT BUTTER & HERSHEY'S KISSES° PIE

WHITE CHIP FRUIT TART

$\frac{3}{4}$ cup (1$\frac{1}{2}$ sticks) butter or margarine, softened
$\frac{1}{2}$ cup powdered sugar
1$\frac{1}{2}$ cups all-purpose flour
2 cups (12-ounce package) HERSHEY'S Premier White Chips
$\frac{1}{4}$ cup whipping cream
1 package (8 ounces) cream cheese, softened
Fruit Topping (recipe follows)
Assorted fresh fruit, sliced

1. Heat oven to 300°F.

2. Beat butter and powdered sugar in small bowl until smooth; blend in flour. Press mixture onto bottom and up side of 12-inch round pizza pan. Flute edge, if desired.

3. Bake 20 to 25 minutes or until lightly browned; cool completely.

4. Place white chips and whipping cream in medium microwave-safe bowl. Microwave at HIGH (100%) 1 to 1$\frac{1}{2}$ minutes or until chips are melted and mixture is smooth when stirred. Beat in cream cheese. Spread on cooled crust. Prepare Fruit Topping. Arrange fruit over chip mixture; carefully pour or brush topping over fruit. Cover; refrigerate assembled tart until just before serving.   *Makes 10 to 12 servings*

FRUIT TOPPING

$\frac{1}{4}$ cup sugar
1 tablespoon cornstarch
$\frac{1}{2}$ cup pineapple juice
$\frac{1}{2}$ teaspoon lemon juice

Stir together sugar and cornstarch in small saucepan; stir in juices. Cook over medium heat, stirring constantly, until thickened; cool.

WHITE CHIP FRUIT TART

59

PEANUT BUTTER AND CHOCOLATE MOUSSE PIE

1 (9-inch) pie crust, baked and cooled
1²⁄₃ cups (10-ounce package) REESE'S® Peanut Butter Chips, divided
1 package (3 ounces) cream cheese, softened
¼ cup powdered sugar
⅓ cup plus 2 tablespoons milk, divided
1 teaspoon unflavored gelatin
1 tablespoon cold water
2 tablespoons boiling water
½ cup sugar
⅓ cup HERSHEY'S Cocoa
1 cup (½ pint) cold whipping cream
1 teaspoon vanilla extract

1. Place 1½ cups peanut butter chips in medium microwave-safe bowl. Microwave at HIGH (100%) 1 minute or until chips are melted and smooth when stirred. Beat cream cheese, powdered sugar and ⅓ cup milk in medium bowl until smooth. Add melted chips; beat well. Beat in remaining 2 tablespoons milk. Spread into cooled crust.

2. Sprinkle gelatin over cold water in small bowl; let stand 1 minute to soften. Add boiling water; stir until gelatin is completely dissolved. Cool slightly. Combine sugar and cocoa in medium bowl; add whipping cream and vanilla. Beat on medium speed of mixer until stiff; pour in gelatin mixture, beating until well blended. Spoon into crust over peanut butter layer. Refrigerate several hours. Garnish with remaining chips. Cover; refrigerate leftover pie.

Makes 6 to 8 servings

PEANUT BUTTER AND CHOCOLATE MOUSSE PIE

CHERRY-GLAZED CHOCOLATE TORTE

½ cup (1 stick) butter or margarine, melted
1 cup granulated sugar
1 teaspoon vanilla extract
2 eggs
½ cup all-purpose flour
⅓ cup HERSHEY'S Cocoa
¼ teaspoon baking powder
¼ teaspoon salt
1 package (8 ounces) cream cheese, softened
1 cup powdered sugar
1 cup frozen non-dairy whipped topping, thawed
1 can (21 ounces) cherry pie filling, divided

1. Heat oven to 350°F. Grease bottom of 9-inch springform pan.

2. Stir together butter, sugar and vanilla in large bowl. Add eggs; using spoon, beat well. Stir together flour, cocoa, baking powder and salt; gradually add to egg mixture, beating until well blended. Spread batter into prepared pan.

3. Bake 25 to 30 minutes or until cake is set. (Cake will be fudgey and will not test done.) Remove from oven; cool completely in pan on wire rack.

4. Beat cream cheese and powdered sugar in medium bowl until well blended; gradually fold in whipped topping, blending well. Spread over top of cake. Spread 1 cup cherry pie filling over cream layer; refrigerate several hours. With knife, loosen cake from side of pan; remove side of pan. Cut into wedges; garnish with remaining pie filling. Cover; refrigerate leftover dessert. *Makes 10 to 12 servings*

CHERRY GLAZED CHOCOLATE TORTE

CLASSIC CHOCOLATE CREAM PIE

$2\frac{1}{2}$ bars (1 ounce *each*) HERSHEY'S Unsweetened Baking Chocolate, broken into pieces

3 cups milk, divided

$1\frac{1}{3}$ cups sugar

3 tablespoons all-purpose flour

3 tablespoons cornstarch

$\frac{1}{2}$ teaspoon salt

3 egg yolks

2 tablespoons butter or margarine

$1\frac{1}{2}$ teaspoons vanilla extract

1 baked (9-inch) pie crust, cooled, or 1 (9-inch) crumb crust

Sweetened whipped cream (optional)

1. Combine chocolate and 2 cups milk in medium saucepan; cook over medium heat, stirring constantly, just until mixture boils. Remove from heat and set aside.

2. Stir together sugar, flour, cornstarch and salt in medium bowl. Whisk remaining 1 cup milk into egg yolks in separate bowl; stir into sugar mixture. Gradually add to chocolate mixture. Cook over medium heat, whisking constantly, until mixture boils; boil and stir 1 minute. Remove from heat; stir in butter and vanilla.

3. Pour into prepared crust; press plastic wrap directly onto surface. Cool; refrigerate until well chilled. Top with whipped cream, if desired. *Makes 8 to 10 servings*

TIP

When cutting cream pies, the slices will cut better if the knife is wiped with a damp cloth or paper towel between cuts.

CLASSIC CHOCOLATE CREAM PIE

VIENNESE CHOCOLATE TORTE

¼ cup HERSHEY'S Cocoa

¼ cup boiling water

⅓ cup shortening

¾ cup sugar

½ teaspoon vanilla extract

1 egg

1 cup all-purpose flour

¾ teaspoon baking soda

¼ teaspoon salt

⅔ cup buttermilk or sour milk*

¼ cup seedless black raspberry preserves

Cream Filling (recipe follows)

Cocoa Glaze (page 68)

MOUNDS® Coconut Flakes, toasted

*To sour milk: Use 2 teaspoons white vinegar plus milk to equal ⅔ cup.

1. Heat oven to 350°F. Lightly grease 15½×10½×1-inch jelly-roll pan; line pan with wax paper and lightly grease paper.

2. Stir together cocoa and boiling water in small bowl until smooth; set aside. Beat shortening, sugar and vanilla in medium bowl until creamy; beat in egg. Stir together flour, baking soda and salt; add alternately with buttermilk to shortening mixture. Add reserved cocoa mixture, beating just until blended. Spread batter into pan. Bake 16 to 18 minutes or until wooden pick inserted in center comes out clean. Cool 10 minutes; remove from pan. Remove wax paper; cool completely.

3. Prepare Cream Filling and Cocoa Glaze. Cut cake crosswise into three equal pieces. Place one piece on serving plate; spread 2 tablespoons preserves evenly on top of cake. Spread half of Cream Filling over preserves. Repeat layering. Glaze top of torte with Cocoa Glaze, allowing some to drizzle down sides. Garnish with coconut. Refrigerate several hours. Cover; refrigerate leftover torte. **Makes 10 servings**

CREAM FILLING: Beat 1 cup whipping cream, 2 tablespoons powdered sugar and 1 teaspoon vanilla extract in small bowl until stiff. Makes about 2 cups filling.

continued on page 68

VIENNESE CHOCOLATE TORTE

Viennese Chocolate Torte, continued

COCOA GLAZE

2 tablespoons butter or margarine
2 tablespoons HERSHEY'S Cocoa
2 tablespoons water
1 cup powdered sugar
½ teaspoon vanilla extract

Melt butter in saucepan. Stir in cocoa and water. Cook, stirring constantly, until mixture thickens. *Do not boil.* Remove from heat. Whisk in powdered sugar gradually. Add vanilla and beat with whisk until smooth. Add additional water ½ teaspoon at a time until desired consistency is reached.

CREAMY CHOCOLATE TARTS

⅔ cup HERSHEY'S Semi-Sweet Chocolate Chips
¼ cup milk
1 tablespoon sugar
½ teaspoon vanilla extract
½ cup chilled whipping cream
6 (one 4-ounce package) single-serve graham crusts
Sweetened whipped cream
Sliced fresh fruit or maraschino cherries or chilled cherry pie filling or fresh mint

1. Place chocolate chips, milk and sugar in small microwave-safe bowl. Microwave at HIGH (100%) 1 minute or until milk is hot and chips are melted when stirred. With wire whisk or rotary beater beat until mixture is smooth; stir in vanilla. Cool to room temperature.

2. Beat whipping cream until stiff; carefully fold chocolate mixture into whipped cream until blended. Spoon or pipe into crusts. Cover; refrigerate until set. Top with sweetened whipped cream. Garnish as desired. *Makes 6 servings*

CHOCOLATE CHIPS PECAN TORTE

    1 cup (2 sticks) butter or margarine, melted
1½ cups sugar
1½ teaspoons vanilla extract
    3 eggs, separated and at room temperature
⅔ cup HERSHEY'S Cocoa
½ cup all-purpose flour
    3 tablespoons water
¾ cup finely chopped pecans
⅛ teaspoon cream of tartar
⅛ teaspoon salt
    2 cups (12-ounce package) HERSHEY'S Semi-Sweet Chocolate Chips,
        divided
    Royal Chip Glaze (recipe follows)
    Sweetened whipped cream (optional)
    Pecan halves (optional)

1. Heat oven to 350°F. Line bottom of 9-inch springform pan with foil; butter foil and side of pan.

2. Combine melted butter, sugar and vanilla; beat well. Add egg yolks, one at a time, beating after each addition. Add cocoa, flour and water; beat well. Stir in chopped pecans.

3. Beat egg whites, cream of tartar and salt in small bowl with clean set of beaters until stiff peaks form; carefully fold into chocolate mixture with 1 cup chocolate chips, reserving remaining chips for glaze. Pour mixture into prepared pan.

4. Bake 45 minutes or until top begins to crack slightly. (Cake will not test done in center.) Cool 1 hour. Cover; refrigerate until firm. Loosen cake from side of pan; remove side of pan. Prepare Royal Chip Glaze; pour over cake, allowing to run down sides. With metal spatula, spread glaze evenly on top and sides. Garnish with sweetened whipped cream or pecan halves, if desired. Cover; refrigerate leftover dessert. *Makes 10 to 12 servings*

ROYAL CHIP GLAZE: Combine remaining 1 cup chocolate chips and ¼ cup milk in small saucepan. Cook over very low heat, stirring constantly, until chocolate is melted and mixture is smooth; do not boil. Remove from heat; cool, stirring occasionally, until mixture thickens, about 10 to 15 minutes.

CHOCOLATE MAGIC MOUSSE PIE

1 envelope unflavored gelatin
2 tablespoons cold water
$\frac{1}{4}$ cup boiling water
1 cup sugar
$\frac{1}{2}$ cup HERSHEY'S Cocoa
2 cups (1 pint) cold whipping cream
2 teaspoons vanilla extract
1 packaged graham cracker crumb crust (6 ounces)
   Refrigerated whipped light cream in pressurized can
   HERSHEY'S MINI KISSES® Brand Milk Chocolates

1. Sprinkle gelatin over cold water in small bowl; let stand 2 minutes to soften. Add boiling water; stir until gelatin is completely dissolved and mixture is clear. Cool slightly.

2. Mix sugar and cocoa in large bowl; add whipping cream and vanilla. Beat on medium speed, scraping bottom of bowl often, until mixture is stiff. Pour in gelatin mixture; beat until well blended. Spoon into crust. Refrigerate about 3 hours. Garnish with whipped cream and chocolate pieces. Store, covered, in refrigerator.

Makes 6 to 8 servings

TIP

Powdered gelatin will last indefinitely if it is wrapped airtight and stored in a cool, dry place. It is important to soak gelatin in cold liquid for several minutes (as the recipe directs) before dissolving it, so the gelatin granules soften, swell and dissolve smoothly when heated.

CHOCOLATE MAGIC MOUSSE PIE

FUDGE BROWNIE PIE

2 eggs
1 cup sugar
½ cup (1 stick) butter or margarine, melted
½ cup all-purpose flour
⅓ cup HERSHEY'S Cocoa
¼ teaspoon salt
1 teaspoon vanilla extract
½ cup chopped nuts (optional)
Ice cream
Hot Fudge Sauce (recipe follows)

1. Heat oven to 350°F. Lightly grease 8-inch pie plate.

2. Beat eggs in small bowl; blend in sugar and melted butter. Stir together flour, cocoa and salt; add to butter mixture. Stir in vanilla and nuts, if desired. Pour into prepared pie plate.

3. Bake 25 to 30 minutes or until almost set. (Pie will not test done in center.) Cool; cut into wedges. Serve topped with scoop of ice cream and drizzled with Hot Fudge Sauce.

Makes 6 to 8 servings

HOT FUDGE SAUCE

¾ cup sugar
½ cup HERSHEY'S Cocoa
½ cup plus 2 tablespoons (5-ounce can) evaporated milk
⅓ cup light corn syrup
⅓ cup butter or margarine
1 teaspoon vanilla extract

Stir together sugar and cocoa in small saucepan; blend in evaporated milk and corn syrup. Cook over medium heat, stirring constantly, until mixture boils; boil and stir 1 minute. Remove from heat; stir in butter and vanilla. Serve warm.

Makes about 1¾ cups sauce

FUDGE BROWNIE PIE

EASY CHOCOLATE CREAM-FILLED TORTE

1 frozen pound cake (10¾ ounces), thawed
½ cup powdered sugar
¼ cup HERSHEY'S Cocoa
1 cup (½ pint) cold whipping cream
1 teaspoon vanilla extract
  Chocolate Glaze (recipe follows)
  Sliced almonds (optional)

1. Cut cake horizontally to make 4 layers. Stir together sugar and cocoa in medium bowl. Add whipping cream and vanilla; beat until stiff.

2. Place bottom cake layer on serving platter. Spread ⅓ of the whipped cream mixture on cake layer. Place next cake layer on top of whipped cream mixture; continue layering whipped cream mixture and cake until all have been used.

3. Prepare Chocolate Glaze; spoon over top of cake, allowing to drizzle down sides. Garnish with almonds, if desired. Refrigerate until ready to serve. Cover; refrigerate leftover torte.

Makes 8 to 10 servings

Prep Time: 20 minutes
Chill Time: 30 minutes

CHOCOLATE GLAZE

2 tablespoons butter or margarine
2 tablespoons HERSHEY'S Cocoa
2 tablespoons water
1 cup powdered sugar
¼ to ½ teaspoon almond extract

1. Melt butter in small saucepan over low heat. Add cocoa and water. Cook, stirring constantly, until smooth and slightly thickened. Do not boil.

2. Remove from heat. Gradually add powdered sugar and almond extract, beating with whisk until smooth.

Makes about ½ cup glaze

EASY CHOCOLATE CREAM-FILLED TORTE

UPSIDE-DOWN HOT FUDGE SUNDAE PIE

$2/3$ cup butter or margarine

$1/3$ cup HERSHEY'S Cocoa

2 eggs

$1/4$ cup milk

1 teaspoon vanilla extract

1 cup packed light brown sugar

$1/2$ cup granulated sugar

1 tablespoon all-purpose flour

$1/8$ teaspoon salt

1 unbaked 9-inch pie crust

2 bananas, peeled and thinly sliced

Ice cream, any flavor

Whipped topping

1. Heat oven to 350°F.

2. Melt butter in medium saucepan over low heat. Add cocoa; stir until smooth. Remove from heat. Stir together eggs, milk and vanilla in small bowl. Add egg mixture to cocoa mixture; stir with whisk until smooth and slightly thickened. Add brown sugar, granulated sugar, flour and salt; stir with whisk until smooth. Pour mixture into unbaked crust.

3. Bake 30 to 35 minutes until edge is set. (Center will be soft.) Cool about 2 hours. Just before serving, top each serving with banana slices, ice cream and whipped topping.

Makes 8 servings

TIP

Ice cream is often too hard to scoop when it's right out of the freezer. So when everybody is screaming for ice cream, here's how to serve it up fast! Place a 1-quart container of hard-packed ice cream in the microwave and heat at MEDIUM (50% power) about 20 seconds or just until softened.

UPSIDE-DOWN HOT FUDGE SUNDAE PIE

HERSHEY'S WHITE AND DARK CHOCOLATE FUDGE TORTE

     1 cup (2 sticks) butter or margarine, melted
 1½ cups sugar
     1 teaspoon vanilla extract
     3 eggs, separated
 ⅔ cup HERSHEY'S Cocoa
 ½ cup all-purpose flour
     3 tablespoons water
     2 cups (12-ounce package) HERSHEY'S Premier White Chips, divided
 ⅛ teaspoon cream of tartar
     Satiny Glaze (recipe follows)
     White Decorator Drizzle (page 80)

1. Heat oven to 350°F. Line bottom of 9-inch springform pan with foil; grease foil and side of pan.

2. Combine butter, sugar and vanilla in large bowl; beat well. Add egg yolks, one at a time, beating well after each addition. Blend in cocoa, flour and water. Stir in 1⅔ cups white chips. Reserve remaining chips for drizzle. Beat egg whites with cream of tartar in small bowl until stiff peaks form; fold into chocolate mixture. Pour batter into prepared pan.

3. Bake 45 minutes or until top begins to crack slightly. (Cake will not test done in center.) Cool 1 hour. Cover; refrigerate until firm. Remove side of pan. Prepare Satiny Glaze and White Decorator Drizzle. Pour prepared glaze over torte; spread evenly over top and side. Decorate top of torte with prepared drizzle.* Cover; refrigerate until serving time. Refrigerate leftover torte. *Makes 10 to 12 servings*

To decorate, drizzle with spoon or place in pastry bag with writing tip.

SATINY GLAZE

     1 cup HERSHEY'S Semi-Sweet Chocolate Chips
 ¼ cup whipping cream

Place chocolate chips and whipping cream in small microwave-safe bowl. Microwave at HIGH (100%) 1 minute; stir. If necessary, microwave at HIGH an additional 15 seconds at a time, stirring after each heating, just until chips are melted when stirred. Cool until lukewarm and slightly thickened. *Makes about ¾ cup glaze*

continued on page 80

HERSHEY.'S WHITE AND DARK CHOCOLATE FUDGE TORTE

Hershey's White and Dark Chocolate Fudge Torte, continued

WHITE DECORATOR DRIZZLE

$\frac{1}{3}$ cup HERSHEY'S Premier White Chips (reserved from torte)

2 teaspoons shortening (do *not* use butter, margarine, spread or oil)

Place white chips and shortening in small microwave-safe bowl. Microwave at HIGH (100%) 20 to 30 seconds; stir. If necessary, microwave at HIGH an additional 15 seconds at a time, stirring after each heating, just until chips are melted when stirred.

CHOCOLATE PECAN PIE

1 cup sugar

$\frac{1}{3}$ cup HERSHEY'S Cocoa

3 eggs, lightly beaten

$\frac{3}{4}$ cup light corn syrup

1 tablespoon butter or margarine, melted

1 teaspoon vanilla extract

1 cup pecan halves

1 unbaked (9-inch pie) crust

Whipped topping (optional)

1. Heat oven to 350°F.

2. Stir together sugar and cocoa in medium bowl. Add eggs, corn syrup, butter and vanilla; stir until well blended. Stir in pecans. Pour into unbaked pie crust.

3. Bake 60 minutes or until set. Remove to wire rack and cool completely. Garnish with whipped topping, if desired.   *Makes 8 servings*

FLOURLESS CHOCOLATE TORTE

1¼ cups (2½ sticks) butter
¾ cup HERSHEY'S Cocoa
2 cups sugar, divided
6 eggs, separated
¼ cup water
1 teaspoon vanilla extract
1 cup blanched sliced almonds, toasted and ground*
½ cup plain dry bread crumbs
Mocha Cream (recipe follows)

*To toast almonds: Heat oven to 350°F. Place almonds in single layer in shallow baking pan. Bake 7 to 8 minutes, stirring occasionally, until light brown. Cool completely.

1. Heat oven to 350°F. Grease and flour 9-inch springform pan.

2. Melt butter in saucepan over low heat. Add cocoa and 1½ cups sugar; stir until smooth. Cool to room temperature.

3. Beat egg yolks in large bowl until thick. Gradually beat in chocolate mixture; stir in water and vanilla. Combine ground almonds and bread crumbs; stir into chocolate mixture. Beat egg whites until foamy; gradually add remaining ½ cup sugar, beating until soft peaks form. Fold about one-third of egg whites into chocolate. Fold chocolate into remaining egg whites. Pour into prepared pan.

4. Bake 50 to 60 minutes or until wooden pick inserted in center comes out clean. Cool 10 minutes. Loosen cake from side of pan; remove pan. Cool completely. Spread Mocha Cream over top. Sift with cocoa just before serving. Store covered in refrigerator.

Makes 10 servings

MOCHA CREAM: Combine 1 cup (½ pint) cold whipping cream, 2 tablespoons powdered sugar, 1½ teaspoons instant coffee granules dissolved in 1 teaspoon water, and ½ teaspoon vanilla extract in medium bowl; beat until stiff. Makes about 2 cups.

CHOCOLATE & VANILLA SWIRL TART

Tart Shell (recipe follows)
$^2/_3$ cup HERSHEY¦S Semi-Sweet Chocolate Chips
$^1/_2$ cup milk, divided
2 tablespoons sugar
$^1/_2$ teaspoon unflavored gelatin
1 tablespoon cold water
$^2/_3$ cup HERSHEY¦S Premier White Chips
1 teaspoon vanilla extract
1 cup ($^1/_2$ pint) cold whipping cream

1. Prepare Tart Shell.

2. Place chocolate chips, $^1/_4$ cup milk and sugar in small microwave-safe bowl. Microwave at HIGH (100%) 1 minute; stir. If necessary, microwave at HIGH an additional 15 seconds at a time, stirring after each heating, just until chips are melted when stirred. Cool about 20 minutes.

3. Sprinkle gelatin over water in small cup; let stand 2 minutes to soften. Place white chips and remaining $^1/_4$ cup milk in second small microwave-safe bowl. Microwave at HIGH 1 minute; stir. Add gelatin mixture and vanilla; stir until gelatin is dissolved. Cool about 20 minutes.

4. Beat whipping cream in small bowl on high speed of mixer until stiff; fold 1 cup whipped cream into vanilla mixture. Fold remaining whipped cream into chocolate mixture. Alternately, spoon chocolate and vanilla mixtures into prepared tart shell; swirl with knife for marbled effect. Refrigerate until firm. Cover; refrigerate leftover tart.

Makes 8 to 10 servings

TART SHELL

$^1/_2$ cup (1 stick) butter (do *not* use margarine), softened
2 tablespoons sugar
2 egg yolks
1 cup all-purpose flour

1. Heat oven to 375°F. Grease bottom and sides of fluted 8- or 9-inch tart pan.

2. Beat butter and sugar in small bowl until blended. Add egg yolks; mix well. Stir in flour until mixture is crumbly. Press onto bottom and up sides of prepared pan. (If dough is sticky, sprinkle with 1 tablespoon flour.) Prick bottom with fork to prevent puffing.

3. Bake 8 to 10 minutes or until lightly browned. Cool completely.

CHOCOLATE & VANILLA SWIRL TART

MINI CHOCOLATE PIES

1 package (4-serving size) vanilla cook & serve pudding and pie filling mix*
1 cup HERSHEY'S MINI CHIPS™ Semi-Sweet Chocolate Chips
1 package (4 ounces) single serve graham cracker crusts (6 crusts)
Whipped topping
Additional MINI CHIPS™ Semi-Sweet Chocolate Chips

*Do not use instant pudding mix.

1. Prepare pudding and pie filling mix as directed on package; remove from heat. Immediately add 1 cup mini chocolate chips; stir until melted. Cool 5 minutes, stirring occasionally.

2. Pour filling into crusts; press plastic wrap directly onto surface. Refrigerate several hours or until firm. Garnish with whipped topping and small chocolate chips.

Makes 6 servings

Prep Time: 5 minutes
Cook Time: 10 minutes
Cool Time: 5 minutes
Chill Time: 2 hours

TIP

Be creative with these adorable pies.
Top them with semi-sweet chocolate, white chocolate or peanut butter chips or use all three flavors.

MINI CHOCOLATE PIES

3

COOKIES, BROWNIES & BARS

CINNAMON CHIPS GEMS

1 cup (2 sticks) butter or margarine, softened
2 packages (3 ounces *each*) cream cheese, softened
2 cups all-purpose flour
$\frac{1}{2}$ cup sugar
$\frac{1}{3}$ cup ground toasted almonds
2 eggs
1 can (14 ounces) sweetened condensed milk
1 teaspoon vanilla extract
$1\frac{1}{3}$ cups HERSHEY'S Cinnamon Chips, divided

1. Beat butter and cream cheese in large bowl until well blended; stir in flour, sugar and almonds. Cover; refrigerate about 1 hour.

2. Divide dough into 4 equal parts. Shape each part into 12 smooth balls. Place each ball in small muffin cup ($1\frac{3}{4}$ inches in diameter); press evenly on bottom and up side of each cup.

3. Heat oven to 375°F. Beat eggs in small bowl. Add sweetened condensed milk and vanilla; mix well. Place 7 cinnamon chips in bottom of each cookie shell; fill a generous $\frac{3}{4}$ full with sweetened condensed milk mixture.

4. Bake 18 to 20 minutes or until tops are puffed and just beginning to turn golden brown. Cool 3 minutes. Sprinkle about 15 chips on top of each cookie. Cool completely in pan on wire rack. Remove from pan using small metal spatula or sharp knife. Store tightly covered at room temperature.   *Makes 4 dozen cookies*

TIP

Read the entire recipe before beginning
to make sure you have all the necessary
ingredients and baking utensils.

CINNAMON CHIPS GEMS

MINI BROWNIE CUPS

¼ cup (½ stick) 60% corn oil spread
2 egg whites
1 egg
¾ cup sugar
⅔ cup all-purpose flour
⅓ cup HERSHEY'S Cocoa
½ teaspoon baking powder
¼ teaspoon salt
Mocha Glaze (recipe follows)

1. Heat oven to 350°F. Line small muffin cups (1¾ inches in diameter) with paper baking cups or spray with vegetable cooking spray.

2. Melt corn oil spread in small saucepan over low heat; cool slightly. Beat egg whites and egg with electric mixer on medium speed in small bowl until foamy; gradually add sugar, beating until slightly thickened and light in color. Stir together flour, cocoa, baking powder and salt; gradually add to egg mixture, beating until blended. Gradually add corn oil spread, beating just until blended. Fill muffin cups ⅔ full with batter.

3. Bake 15 to 18 minutes or until wooden pick inserted in center comes out clean. Remove from pan to wire rack. Cool completely. Prepare Mocha Glaze; drizzle over tops of brownie cups. Let stand until glaze is set. *Makes 24 servings*

MOCHA GLAZE

¼ cup powdered sugar
¾ teaspoon HERSHEY'S Cocoa
¼ teaspoon powdered instant coffee
2 teaspoons hot water
¼ teaspoon vanilla extract

Stir together powdered sugar and cocoa in small bowl. Dissolve coffee in water; gradually add to sugar mixture, stirring until well blended. Stir in vanilla.

Makes about 2 tablespoons glaze

MINI BROWNIE CUPS

HERSHEY'S TRIPLE CHOCOLATE COOKIES

48 HERSHEY'S KISSES® Brand Milk Chocolates or HERSHEY'S KISSES® Brand WITH ALMONDS Chocolates
½ cup (1 stick) butter or margarine, softened
¾ cup granulated sugar
¾ cup packed light brown sugar
1 teaspoon vanilla extract
2 eggs
1 tablespoon milk
2¼ cups all-purpose flour
⅓ cup HERSHEY'S Cocoa
1 teaspoon baking soda
½ teaspoon salt
1 cup HERSHEY'S Semi-Sweet Chocolate Chips

1. Remove wrappers from chocolates. Heat oven to 350°F.

2. Beat butter, granulated sugar, brown sugar and vanilla with electric mixer on medium speed in large bowl until well blended. Add eggs and milk; beat well.

3. Stir together flour, cocoa, baking soda and salt; gradually beat into butter mixture, beating until well blended. Stir in chocolate chips. Shape dough into 1-inch balls. Place on ungreased cookie sheet.

4. Bake 10 to 11 minutes or until set. Gently press a chocolate into center of each cookie. Remove to wire rack and cool completely. *Makes about 4 dozen cookies*

VARIATION: For vanilla cookies, omit cocoa and add an additional ⅓ cup all-purpose flour.

HERSHEY'S TRIPLE CHOCOLATE COOKIES

PEANUT BUTTER GLAZED CHOCOLATE BARS

¾ cup (1½ sticks) butter or margarine
½ cup HERSHEY'S Cocoa
1½ cups sugar
1½ teaspoons vanilla extract
3 eggs
1¼ cups all-purpose flour
¼ teaspoon baking powder
    Peanut Butter Filling and Glaze (recipe follows)
    Chocolate Drizzle (recipe follows)

1. Heat oven to 350°F. Line 15½×10½×1-inch jelly-roll pan with foil; grease foil.

2. Melt butter in medium saucepan over low heat. Add cocoa; stir constantly until smooth. Remove from heat; stir in sugar and vanilla. Beat in eggs, one at a time, until well combined. Stir in flour and baking powder. Spread batter evenly into prepared pan.

3. Bake 14 to 16 minutes or until top springs back when touched lightly in center. Remove from oven; cool 2 minutes. Invert onto wire rack. Peel off foil; turn right side up on wire rack to cool completely.

4. Prepare Peanut Butter Filling and Glaze. Cut brownie in half; spread half of glaze evenly on one half. Top with second half; spread with remaining glaze. Cool until glaze is set. Prepare Chocolate Drizzle; drizzle over glaze. After chocolate is set, cut into bars.

Makes about 40 bars

PEANUT BUTTER FILLING AND GLAZE: Combine ⅓ cup sugar and ⅓ cup water in small saucepan; cook over medium heat to boiling. Remove from heat; immediately add 1⅔ cups (10-ounce package) REESE'S® Peanut Butter Chips. Stir until melted. Cool slightly. Makes about 1⅓ cups glaze.

CHOCOLATE DRIZZLE: Place ⅓ cup HERSHEY'S Semi-Sweet Chocolate Chips and 1 teaspoon shortening (do *not* use butter, margarine, spread or oil) in small microwave-safe bowl. Microwave at HIGH (100%) 30 seconds to 1 minute or until chips are melted and mixture is smooth when stirred.

PEANUT BUTTER GLAZED CHOCOLATE BARS

ULTIMATE CHOCOLATE BROWNIES

¾ cup HERSHEY'S Cocoa

½ teaspoon baking soda

⅔ cup butter or margarine, melted and divided

½ cup boiling water

2 cups sugar

2 eggs

1⅓ cups all-purpose flour

1 teaspoon vanilla extract

¼ teaspoon salt

1 cup HERSHEY'S Semi-Sweet Chocolate Chips

One-Bowl Buttercream Frosting (recipe follows)

1. Heat oven to 350°F. Grease 13×9×2-inch baking pan or two 8-inch square baking pans.

2. Stir together cocoa and baking soda in large bowl; stir in ⅓ cup melted butter. Add boiling water; stir until mixture thickens. Stir in sugar, eggs and remaining ⅓ cup butter; stir until smooth. Add flour, vanilla and salt; blend completely. Stir in chocolate chips. Pour into prepared pan(s).

3. Bake 35 to 40 minutes for rectangular pan, 30 to 35 minutes for square pans or until brownies begin to pull away from sides of pan. Cool completely in pan on wire rack. Meanwhile, prepare One-Bowl Buttercream Frosting. Frost brownies; cut into squares.

Makes about 36 brownies

ONE-BOWL BUTTERCREAM FROSTING

6 tablespoons butter or margarine, softened

2⅔ cups powdered sugar

½ cup HERSHEY'S Cocoa

⅓ cup milk

1 teaspoon vanilla extract

Beat butter in medium bowl. Add powdered sugar and cocoa alternately with milk, beating to spreading consistency (additional milk may be needed). Stir in vanilla.

Makes about 2 cups frosting

SECRET KISSES® COOKIES

   1 cup (2 sticks) butter or margarine, softened
   ½ cup granulated sugar
   1 teaspoon vanilla extract
  1¾ cups all-purpose flour
   1 cup finely chopped walnuts or almonds
  36 HERSHEY'S KISSES® Brand Milk Chocolates or HERSHEY'S KISSES® Brand
      WITH ALMONDS Chocolates
   Powdered sugar

1. Beat butter, granulated sugar and vanilla with electric mixer on medium speed in large bowl until fluffy. Add flour and walnuts; mix on low speed until well blended. Cover; refrigerate 1 to 2 hours or until dough is firm enough to handle.

2. Remove wrappers from chocolates. Heat oven to 375°F. Using about 1 tablespoon dough for each cookie, shape dough around each chocolate; shape into balls. (Be sure to cover each chocolate piece completely.) Place on ungreased cookie sheet.

3. Bake 10 to 12 minutes or until cookies are set but not browned. Cool slightly; remove to wire rack. While still slightly warm, roll in powdered sugar. Cool completely. Store in tightly covered container. Roll again in powdered sugar just before serving.

Makes 3 dozen cookies

TIP

For a variation on this tasty recipe, sift together 1 tablespoon HERSHEY'S Cocoa with ⅓ cup powdered sugar. After removing cookies from oven, roll in cocoa mixture instead of powdered sugar.

CHEWY TOFFEE ALMOND BARS

1 cup (2 sticks) butter, softened
$\frac{1}{2}$ cup sugar
2 cups all-purpose flour
$1\frac{1}{3}$ cups (8-ounce package) HEATH® BITS 'O BRICKLE® Almond Toffee Bits
$\frac{3}{4}$ cup light corn syrup
1 cup sliced almonds, divided
$\frac{3}{4}$ cup MOUNDS® Sweetened Coconut Flakes, divided

1. Heat oven to 350°F. Grease sides of 13×9×2-inch baking pan.

2. Beat butter and sugar with electric mixer on medium speed in large bowl until fluffy. Gradually add flour, beating until well blended. Press dough evenly into prepared pan. Bake 15 to 20 minutes or until edges are lightly browned.

3. Meanwhile, combine toffee bits and corn syrup in medium saucepan. Cook over medium heat, stirring constantly, until toffee is melted (about 10 to 12 minutes). Stir in $\frac{1}{2}$ cup almonds and $\frac{1}{2}$ cup coconut. Spread toffee mixture to within $\frac{1}{4}$ inch of edges of crust. Sprinkle remaining $\frac{1}{2}$ cup almonds and remaining $\frac{1}{4}$ cup coconut over top.

4. Bake an additional 15 minutes or until bubbly. Cool completely in pan on wire rack. Cut into bars.

Makes 36 bars

TIP

Most bar cookies should cool in the pan on a wire rack until barely warm before cutting into bars or squares. To make serving easy, remove a corner piece first; then remove the rest.

CHEWY TOFFEE ALMOND BARS

REESE'S® PEANUT BUTTER AND MILK CHOCOLATE CHIP TASSIES

$\frac{3}{4}$ cup (1$\frac{1}{2}$ sticks) butter, softened

1 package (3 ounces) cream cheese, softened

1$\frac{1}{2}$ cups all-purpose flour

$\frac{3}{4}$ cup sugar, divided

1 egg, lightly beaten

2 tablespoons butter or margarine, melted

$\frac{1}{4}$ teaspoon lemon juice

$\frac{1}{4}$ teaspoon vanilla extract

1$\frac{3}{4}$ cups (11-ounce package) REESE'S® Peanut Butter and Milk Chocolate Chips, divided

2 teaspoons shortening (do not use butter, margarine, spread or oil)

1. Beat $\frac{3}{4}$ cup butter and cream cheese with electric mixer on medium speed in medium bowl until well blended; add flour and $\frac{1}{4}$ cup sugar, beating until well blended. Cover; refrigerate about 1 hour or until dough is firm. Shape dough into 1-inch balls; press balls onto bottoms and up sides of 36 small muffin cups (1$\frac{3}{4}$ inches in diameter).

2. Heat oven to 350°F. Combine egg, remaining $\frac{1}{2}$ cup sugar, melted butter, lemon juice and vanilla in small bowl; stir until smooth. Set aside $\frac{1}{3}$ cup chips; add remainder to egg mixture. Evenly fill muffin cups with egg mixture.

3. Bake 20 to 25 minutes or until filling is set and lightly browned. Cool completely; remove from pan to wire rack.

4. Combine reserved $\frac{1}{3}$ cup chips and shortening in small microwave-safe bowl. Microwave at HIGH (100%) 30 seconds; stir. If necessary, microwave additional 15 seconds at a time, stirring after each heating, until chips are melted and mixture is smooth when stirred. Drizzle over tops of tassies. *Makes 3 dozen cookies*

REESE'S® PEANUT BUTTER AND MILK CHOCOLATE CHIP TASSIES

WHITE CHIP LEMON STREUSEL BARS

1 can (14 ounces) sweetened condensed milk (not evaporated milk)
½ cup lemon juice
1 teaspoon freshly grated lemon peel
2 cups (12-ounce package) HERSHEY'S Premier White Chips, divided
⅔ cup butter or margarine, softened
1 cup packed light brown sugar
1½ cups all-purpose flour
1½ cups regular rolled or quick-cooking oats
¾ cup toasted pecan pieces*
1 teaspoon baking powder
½ teaspoon salt
1 egg
½ teaspoon shortening (do *not* use butter, margarine spread or oil)

To toast pecans: Heat oven to 350°F. Spread pecans in thin layer in shallow baking pan. Bake, stirring occasionally, 7 to 8 minutes or until golden brown; cool.

1. Heat oven to 350°F. Lightly grease 13×9×2-inch baking pan. Combine sweetened condensed milk, lemon juice and lemon peel in medium bowl; set aside. Measure out ¼ cup and ⅓ cup white chips; set aside. Add remaining white chips to lemon mixture.

2. Beat butter and brown sugar with electric mixer on medium speed in large bowl until well blended. Stir together flour, oats, pecans, baking powder and salt; add to butter mixture, blending well. Set aside 1⅔ cups oats mixture. Add egg to remaining oats mixture, blending until crumbly; press onto bottom of prepared pan. Gently spoon lemon mixture on top, spreading evenly. Add reserved ⅓ cup white chips to reserved oats mixture. Sprinkle over lemon layer, pressing down lightly.

3. Bake 20 to 25 minutes or until lightly browned. Cool in pan on wire rack. Place remaining ¼ cup white chips and shortening in small microwave-safe bowl. Microwave at HIGH (100%) 30 seconds or until chips are melted and mixture is smooth when stirred. Drizzle over baked bars. Allow drizzle to set; cut into bars.   *Makes 36 bars*

WHITE CHIP LEMON STREUSEL BARS

REESE'S® PEANUT BUTTER AND MILK CHOCOLATE CHIP STUDDED OATMEAL COOKIES

1 cup (2 sticks) butter or margarine, softened
1 cup packed light brown sugar
$\frac{1}{3}$ cup granulated sugar
2 eggs
$1\frac{1}{2}$ teaspoons vanilla extract
$1\frac{1}{2}$ cups all-purpose flour
1 teaspoon baking soda
$\frac{1}{2}$ teaspoon salt
$\frac{1}{2}$ teaspoon ground cinnamon (optional)
$2\frac{1}{2}$ cups quick-cooking oats
$1\frac{3}{4}$ cups (11-ounce package) REESE'S® Peanut Butter and Milk Chocolate Chips

1. Heat oven to 350°F.

2. Beat butter, brown sugar and granulated sugar in bowl until creamy. Add eggs and vanilla; beat well. Combine flour, baking soda, salt and cinnamon, if desired; add to butter mixture, beating well. Stir in oats and chips (batter will be stiff). Drop by rounded teaspoons onto ungreased cookie sheet.

3. Bake 10 to 12 minutes or until lightly browned. Cool 1 minute; remove from cookie sheet to wire rack.   *Makes about 4 dozen*

BAR VARIATION: Spread batter into lightly greased 13×9×2-inch baking pan or $15\frac{1}{2}$×$10\frac{1}{2}$×1-inch jelly-roll pan. Bake at 350°F. for 20 to 25 minutes or until golden brown. Cool; cut into bars. Makes about 3 dozen bars.

REESE'S® PEANUT BUTTER AND MILK CHOCOLATE CHIP STUDDED OATMEAL COOKIES

CHEWY CHOCOLATE-CINNAMON COOKIES

6 tablespoons butter or margarine, softened
$2/3$ cup packed light brown sugar
3 tablespoons plus $1/4$ cup granulated sugar, divided
$1/4$ cup light corn syrup
1 egg
1 teaspoon vanilla extract
1 teaspoon baking soda
$1 1/2$ cups all-purpose flour
$1/3$ cup HERSHEY'S Cocoa
$1/4$ to $1/2$ teaspoon ground cinnamon

1. Heat oven to 350°F. Spray cookie sheet with nonstick cooking spray.

2. Beat butter until creamy. Add brown sugar and 3 tablespoons granulated sugar; beat until blended. Add corn syrup, egg, vanilla and baking soda; beat well.

3. Stir together flour and cocoa; beat into butter mixture. If batter becomes too stiff, use wooden spoon to stir in remaining flour. Cover; refrigerate about 30 minutes, if necessary, until batter is firm enough to shape. Shape dough into 1-inch balls. Combine remaining $1/4$ cup granulated sugar and cinnamon; roll balls in mixture. Place balls 2 inches apart on prepared cookie sheet.

4. Bake 9 to 10 minutes or until cookies are set and tops are cracked. Cool slightly; remove from cookie sheet to wire rack. Cool completely. *Makes about 40 cookies*

COCOA COCONUT BROWNIES

$1/2$ cup (1 stick) butter or margarine, melted
1 cup sugar
1 teaspoon vanilla extract
2 eggs
$1/2$ cup all-purpose flour
$1/3$ cup HERSHEY'S Cocoa
$1/4$ teaspoon baking powder
$1/4$ teaspoon salt
1 cup MOUNDS™ Sweetened Coconut Flakes, divided

1. Heat oven to 350°F. Grease 8-inch square baking pan.

2. Stir together butter, sugar and vanilla in medium bowl. Add eggs; beat well with

spoon. Stir together flour, cocoa, baking powder and salt; gradually add to egg mixture, beating until well blended. Stir in ³⁄₄ cup coconut. Spread batter evenly into prepared pan. Sprinkle remaining ¹⁄₄ cup coconut over top.

3. Bake 25 to 30 minutes or until brownies begin to pull away from sides of pan. Cool completely in pan on wire rack. Cut into squares.   *Makes about 16 brownies*

REALLY CHOCOLATE CHOCOLATE CHIP COOKIES

        6 tablespoons butter or margarine, softened
        6 tablespoons butter flavored shortening
    ²⁄₃ cup packed light brown sugar
    ¹⁄₂ cup granulated sugar
        2 eggs
        2 tablespoons milk
        2 teaspoons vanilla extract
        1 cup all-purpose flour
    ¹⁄₂ cup HERSHEY'S Cocoa
    ¹⁄₂ teaspoon baking soda
    ¹⁄₂ teaspoon salt
        2 cups (12-ounce package) HERSHEY'S SPECIAL DARK® Chocolate Chips
        1 cup chopped nuts
        Powdered sugar (optional)

1. Heat oven to 350°F.

2. Beat butter and shortening with electric mixer on medium speed in large bowl until well blended. Add brown sugar and granulated sugar; beat thoroughly. Add egg, milk and vanilla, beating until well blended.

3. Stir together flour, cocoa, baking soda and salt; gradually beat into butter mixture. Stir in chocolate chips and nuts. Drop by teaspoons onto ungreased cookie sheet.

4. Bake 10 to 12 minutes or until edges are set. Cool slightly. Remove to wire rack and cool completely. Sprinkle with powdered sugar, if desired.

Makes about 5 dozen cookies

PEANUT BUTTER FUDGE BROWNIE BARS

    1 cup (2 sticks) butter or margarine, melted
1½ cups sugar
    2 eggs
    1 teaspoon vanilla extract
1¼ cups all-purpose flour
 ⅔ cup HERSHEY'S Cocoa
 ¼ cup milk
1¼ cups chopped pecans or walnuts, divided
 ½ cup (1 stick) butter or margarine
1⅔ cups (10-ounce package) REESE'S® Peanut Butter Chips
    1 can (14 ounces) sweetened condensed milk (not evaporated milk)
 ¼ cup HERSHEY'S Semi-Sweet Chocolate Chips

1. Heat oven to 350°F. Grease 13×9×2-inch baking pan.

2. Beat melted butter, sugar, eggs and vanilla with electric mixer on medium speed in large bowl until well blended. Add flour, cocoa and milk; beat until blended. Stir in 1 cup nuts. Spread in prepared pan.

3. Bake 25 to 30 minutes or just until edges begin to pull away from sides of pan. Cool completely in pan on wire rack.

4. Melt ½ cup butter and peanut butter chips in medium saucepan over low heat, stirring constantly. Add sweetened condensed milk; stirring until smooth; pour over baked layer.

5. Place chocolate chips in small microwave-safe bowl. Microwave at HIGH (100%) 45 seconds or just until chips are melted when stirred. Drizzle bars with melted chocolate; sprinkle with remaining ¼ cup nuts. Refrigerate 1 hour or until firm. Cut into bars. Cover; refrigerate leftover bars.

Makes 36 bars

PEANUT BUTTER FUDGE BROWNIE BARS

HERSHEY'S DOUBLE CHOCOLATE MINI KISSES COOKIES

1 cup (2 sticks) butter or margarine, softened
1½ cups sugar
2 eggs
2 teaspoons vanilla extract
2 cups all-purpose flour
⅔ cup HERSHEY'S Cocoa
¾ teaspoon baking soda
¼ teaspoon salt
1¾ cups (10-ounce package) HERSHEY'S MINI KISSES® Brand Milk Chocolates
½ cup coarsely chopped nuts (optional)

1. Heat oven to 350°F.

2. Beat butter, sugar, eggs and vanilla with electric mixer on medium speed in large bowl until light and fluffy. Stir together flour, cocoa, baking soda and salt; add to butter mixture, beating until well blended. Stir in chocolates and nuts, if desired. Drop by tablespoonfuls onto ungreased cookie sheet.

3. Bake 8 to 10 minutes or just until set. Cool slightly. Remove to wire rack and cool completely.

Makes about 3½ dozen cookies

TIP

Space the mounds of dough about 2 inches apart on cookie sheets to allow for spreading unless the recipe directs otherwise.

HERSHEY'S DOUBLE CHOCOLATE MINI KISSES COOKIES

CHOCOLATE ORANGE CHEESECAKE BARS

CRUST

- 1 cup all-purpose flour
- ½ cup packed light brown sugar
- ¼ teaspoon ground cinnamon (optional)
- ⅓ cup shortening
- ½ cup chopped pecans

CHOCOLATE ORANGE FILLING

- 1 package (8 ounces) cream cheese, softened
- ⅔ cup granulated sugar
- ⅓ cup HERSHEY'S Cocoa
- ¼ cup milk
- 1 egg
- 1 teaspoon vanilla extract
- ¼ teaspoon freshly grated orange peel
  Pecan halves (optional)

1. Heat oven to 350°F.

2. For crust, stir together flour, brown sugar and cinnamon, if desired, in large bowl. Cut shortening into flour mixture with pastry blender or two knives until mixture resembles coarse crumbs. Stir in chopped pecans. Reserve ¾ cup flour mixture. Press remaining mixture firmly onto bottom of ungreased 9-inch square baking pan. Bake 10 minutes or until lightly browned.

3. For chocolate orange filling, beat cream cheese and sugar with electric mixer on medium speed in medium bowl until fluffy. Add cocoa, milk, egg, vanilla and orange peel; beat until smooth.

4. Spread filling over warm crust. Sprinkle with reserved flour mixture. Press pecan halves lightly onto top, if desired. Return to oven. Bake 25 to 30 minutes or until lightly browned. Cool; cut into bars. Cover; refrigerate leftover bars. *Makes 24 bars*

CHOCOLATE ORANGE CHEESECAKE BARS

FUDGEY COCONUT CLUSTERS

$5\frac{1}{3}$ cups MOUNDS® Sweetened Coconut Flakes

1 can (14 ounces) sweetened condensed milk (not evaporated milk)

$\frac{2}{3}$ cup HERSHEY'S Cocoa

$\frac{1}{4}$ cup ($\frac{1}{2}$ stick) butter, melted

2 teaspoons vanilla extract

$1\frac{1}{2}$ teaspoons almond extract

HERSHEY'S MINI KISSES® Brand Milk Chocolates or candied cherry halves (optional)

1. Heat oven to 350°F. Line cookie sheets with aluminum foil; generously grease foil with vegetable shortening.

2. Combine coconut, sweetened condensed milk, cocoa, melted butter, vanilla and almond extract in large bowl; mix well. Drop by rounded tablespoons onto prepared cookie sheet.

3. Bake 9 to 11 minutes or just until set; press 3 milk chocolates or candied cherry halves in center of each cookie, if desired. Immediately remove cookies to wire rack and cool completely.

Makes about $2\frac{1}{2}$ dozen cookies

CHOCOLATE CHIP MACAROONS: Omit melted butter and cocoa; stir together other ingredients. Add 1 cup HERSHEY'S MINI CHIPS™ Semi-Sweet Chocolate Chips. Bake 9 to 11 minutes or just until set. Immediately remove to wire rack and cool completely.

TIP

When reusing the same baking sheets for several batches, cool the sheets completely before placing dough on them. Dough will soften and begin to spread on a hot sheet.

FUDGEY COCONUT CLUSTERS

PEANUT BUTTER CUT-OUT COOKIES

½ cup (1 stick) butter or margarine
1 cup REESE'S® Peanut Butter Chips
⅔ cup packed light brown sugar
1 egg
¾ teaspoon vanilla extract
1⅓ cups all-purpose flour
¾ teaspoon baking soda
½ cup finely chopped pecans
Chocolate Chip Glaze (recipe follows)

1. Place butter and peanut butter chips in medium saucepan; cook over low heat, stirring constantly, until melted. Pour into large bowl; add brown sugar, egg and vanilla, beating until well blended. Stir in flour, baking soda and pecans, blending well. Refrigerate 15 to 20 minutes or until firm enough to roll.

2. Heat oven to 350°F.

3. Roll a small portion of dough at a time on lightly floured board, or between 2 pieces of wax paper, to ¼-inch thickness. (Keep remaining dough in refrigerator.) With cookie cutters, cut dough into desired shapes; place on ungreased cookie sheet.

4. Bake 7 to 8 minutes or until almost set (do not overbake). Cool 1 minute; remove from cookie sheet to wire rack. Cool completely. Prepare Chocolate Chip Glaze. Drizzle glaze onto each cookie; allow to set. *Makes about 3 dozen cookies*

CHOCOLATE CHIP GLAZE: Place 1 cup HERSHEY®S Semi-Sweet Chocolate Chips and 1 tablespoon shortening (do *not* use butter, margarine spread or oil) in small microwave-safe bowl. Microwave at HIGH (100%) 1 minute; stir. If necessary, microwave at HIGH an additional 15 seconds at a time, stirring after each heating, just until chips are melted and mixture is smooth.

PEANUT BUTTER CUT-OUT COOKIES

RICH CHOCOLATE CHIP TOFFEE BARS

2⅓ cups all-purpose flour

⅔ cup packed light brown sugar

¾ cup (1½ sticks) butter or margarine

1 egg, lightly beaten

2 cups (12-ounce package) HERSHEY'S Semi-Sweet Chocolate Chips, divided

1 cup coarsely chopped nuts

1 can (14 ounces) sweetened condensed milk (not evaporated milk)

1⅓ cups (8-ounce package) HEATH® BITS 'O BRICKLE® Almond Toffee Bits, divided

1. Heat oven to 350°F. Grease 13×9×2-inch baking pan.

2. Combine flour and brown sugar in large bowl. Cut butter into flour mixture with pastry blender or two knives until mixture resembles coarse crumbs. Add egg; mix well. Stir in 1½ cups chocolate chips and nuts; set aside 1½ cups mixture.

3. Press remaining crumb mixture onto bottom of prepared pan. Bake 10 minutes. Pour sweetened condensed milk evenly over hot crust. Set aside ¼ cup toffee bits. Sprinkle remaining toffee bits over sweetened condensed milk. Sprinkle reserved crumb mixture and remaining ½ cup chocolate chips over top.

4. Bake 25 to 30 minutes or until golden brown. Top with reserved ¼ cup toffee bits. Cool completely in pan on wire rack. Cut into bars. *Makes 48 bars*

ROCKY ROAD TASTY TEAM TREATS

1½ cups finely crushed thin pretzels or pretzel sticks

¾ cup (1½ sticks) butter or margarine, melted

1 can (14 ounces) sweetened condensed milk (not evaporated milk)

1¾ cups (10-ounce package) HERSHEY'S MINI KISSES® Brand Milk Chocolates

3 cups miniature marshmallows

1⅓ cups coarsely chopped pecans or pecan pieces

1. Heat oven to 350°F. Grease bottom and sides of 13×9×2-inch baking pan.

2. Combine pretzels and melted butter in small bowl; press evenly onto bottom of prepared pan. Spread sweetened condensed milk evenly over pretzel layer; layer

evenly with chocolates, marshmallows and pecans, in order. Press down firmly on pecans.

3. Bake 20 to 25 minutes or until lightly browned. Cool completely in pan on wire rack. Cut into bars.

Makes about 36 bars

MARBLED CHEESECAKE BARS

    Chocolate Crust (recipe follows)
3 packages (8 ounces *each*) cream cheese, softened
1 can (14 ounces) sweetened condensed milk (not evaporated milk)
3 eggs
2 teaspoons vanilla extract
2 bars (1 ounce each) HERSHEY'S Unsweetened Baking Chocolate, melted

1. Prepare Chocolate Crust. Heat oven to 300°F.

2. Beat cream cheese in large bowl until fluffy. Gradually add sweetened condensed milk, beating until smooth. Add eggs and vanilla; mix well.

3. Pour half of batter evenly over prepared crust. Stir melted chocolate into remaining batter; drop by teaspoons over vanilla batter. With metal spatula or knife, swirl gently through batter to marble.

4. Bake 45 to 50 minutes or until set. Cool in pan on wire rack. Refrigerate several hours until chilled. Cut into bars. Cover; store leftover bars in refrigerator.

Makes 24 to 36 bars

CHOCOLATE CRUST: Stir together 2 cups vanilla wafer crumbs (about 60 wafers), 1/3 cup HERSHEY'S Cocoa and 1/2 cup powdered sugar. Stir in 1/2 cup (1 stick) melted butter or margarine until well blended. Press mixture firmly into bottom of ungreased 13×9×2-inch baking pan.

Prep Time: 25 minutes
Bake Time: 45 minutes
Cool Time: 1 hour
Chill Time: 2 1/2 hours

BROWNIE CARAMEL PECAN BARS

½ cup sugar

2 tablespoons butter or margarine

2 tablespoons water

2 cups (12-ounce package) HERSHEY'S Semi-Sweet Chocolate Chips, divided

2 eggs

1 teaspoon vanilla extract

⅔ cup all-purpose flour

¼ teaspoon baking soda

¼ teaspoon salt

Caramel Topping (recipe follows)

1 cup pecan pieces

1. Heat oven to 350°F. Line 9-inch square baking pan with foil, extending foil over edges of pan. Grease and flour foil.

2. Combine sugar, butter and water in medium saucepan. Cook over low heat, stirring constantly, until mixture boils. Remove from heat. Immediately add 1 cup chocolate chips; stir until melted. Beat in eggs and vanilla until well blended. Stir together flour, baking soda and salt; stir into chocolate mixture. Spread batter into prepared pan.

3. Bake 15 to 20 minutes or until brownies begin to pull away from sides of pan. Meanwhile, prepare Caramel Topping. Remove brownies from oven; immediately and carefully spread with prepared topping. Sprinkle remaining 1 cup chips and pecans over topping. Cool completely in pan on wire rack, being careful not to disturb chips while soft. Lift out of pan. Cut into bars. *Makes about 16 bars*

CARAMEL TOPPING: Remove wrappers from 25 caramels candies. Combine 2 tablespoons butter or margarine, caramels and ½ tablespoon milk in medium microwave-safe bowl. Microwave at HIGH (100%) 1 minute; stir. Microwave an additional 1 to 2 minutes, stirring every 30 seconds, or until caramels are melted and mixture is smooth when stirred. Use immediately.

BROWNIE CARAMEL PECAN BARS

REESE'S® PEANUT BUTTER AND MILK CHOCOLATE CHIP BROWNIES

³⁄₄ cup HERSHEY'S Cocoa
¹⁄₂ teaspoon baking soda
²⁄₃ cup butter or margarine, melted and divided
¹⁄₂ cup boiling water
2 cups sugar
2 eggs
1¹⁄₃ cups all-purpose flour
1 teaspoon vanilla extract
¹⁄₄ teaspoon salt
1³⁄₄ cups (11-ounce package) REESE'S® Peanut Butter and Milk Chocolate Chips

1. Heat oven to 350°F. Grease 13×9×2-inch baking pan.

2. Stir together cocoa and baking soda in large bowl; stir in ¹⁄₃ cup butter. Add water; stir until mixture thickens. Stir in sugar, eggs and remaining ¹⁄₃ cup butter; stir until smooth. Add flour, vanilla and salt; blend thoroughly. Stir in chips. Pour into prepared pan.

3. Bake 35 to 40 minutes or until brownies begin to pull away from sides of pan. Cool completely in pan on wire rack. Cut into squares. *Makes about 36 brownies*

TIP

For easy removal of brownies and bar cookies (and no cleanup!), line the baking pan with foil and leave at least 3 inches hanging over each end. Use the foil to lift out the treats, place them on a cutting board and carefully remove the foil. Then simply cut them into pieces.

REESE'S® PEANUT BUTTER AND MILK CHOCOLATE CHIP BROWNIES

FILLED CHOCOLATE MERINGUES

2 egg whites, at room temperature
¼ teaspoon cream of tartar
   Dash salt
½ cup sugar
½ teaspoon vanilla extract
2 tablespoons HERSHEY'S Cocoa
   Chocolate-Cheese Filling (recipe follows)
   Raspberries and mint leaves for garnish

1. Heat oven to 275°F. Place parchment paper on cookie sheet.

2. Beat egg whites with cream of tartar and salt in medium bowl until soft peaks form. Beat in sugar, 1 tablespoon at a time, until stiff, glossy peaks form. Fold in vanilla. Sift cocoa over top of egg white mixture; gently fold in cocoa until combined. Drop by tablespoonfuls onto parchment paper. With back of small spoon, make indentation in center of each mound.

3. Bake 45 minutes or until meringue turns a light cream color and feels dry to the touch. Cool slightly; carefully peel meringues off parchment paper; cool completely on wire rack. Prepare Chocolate-Cheese Filling. To serve, spoon or pipe about 2 teaspoons filling into center of each meringue. Garnish each with a raspberry and a mint leaf.
Makes 2 dozen meringues

CHOCOLATE-CHEESE FILLING: Combine 1 cup part-skim ricotta cheese, 2 tablespoons HERSHEY'S Cocoa, 1 tablespoon sugar and ½ teaspoon vanilla extract in food processor; blend until smooth. Cover; refrigerate. Makes 1 cup filling.

FILLED CHOCOLATE MERINGUES

CRANBERRY ORANGE RICOTTA CHEESE BROWNIES

½ cup (1 stick) butter or margarine, melted
¾ cup sugar
1 teaspoon vanilla extract
2 eggs
¾ cup all-purpose flour
½ cup HERSHEY'S Cocoa
½ teaspoon baking powder
½ teaspoon salt
Cheese Filling (recipe follows)

1. Heat oven to 350°F. Grease 9-inch square baking pan. Prepare Cheese Filling; set aside.

2. Stir together butter, sugar and vanilla in medium bowl; add eggs, beating well. Stir together flour, cocoa, baking powder and salt; add to butter mixture, mixing thoroughly. Spread half of chocolate batter in prepared pan. Spread prepared filling over top. Drop remaining chocolate batter by teaspoonfuls onto cheese filling.

3. Bake 40 to 45 minutes or until wooden pick inserted in center comes out clean. Cool completely in pan on wire rack. Cut into squares. Refrigerate leftover brownies.

Makes about 16 brownies

CHEESE FILLING

1 cup ricotta cheese
¼ cup sugar
3 tablespoons whole-berry cranberry sauce
2 tablespoons cornstarch
1 egg
¼ to ½ teaspoon freshly grated orange peel
4 drops red food color (optional)

Beat ricotta cheese, sugar, cranberry sauce, cornstarch and egg in small bowl until smooth. Stir in orange peel and food color, if desired. *Makes about 1¼ cups filling*

CRANBERRY ORANGE RICOTTA CHEESE BROWNIES

REESE'S® CLASSIC PEANUT BUTTER AND MILK CHOCOLATE CHIP COOKIES

2¼ cups all-purpose flour

1 teaspoon baking soda

½ teaspoon salt

1 cup (2 sticks) butter, softened

¾ cup granulated sugar

¾ cup packed light brown sugar

1 teaspoon vanilla extract

2 eggs

1¾ cups (11-ounce package) REESE'S® Peanut Butter and Milk Chocolate Chips

1 cup chopped nuts (optional)

1. Heat oven to 375°F.

2. Stir together flour, baking soda and salt. Beat butter, granulated sugar, brown sugar and vanilla in large bowl with mixer until creamy. Add eggs; beat well. Gradually add flour mixture, beating well. Stir in chips and nuts, if desired. Drop by rounded teaspoons onto ungreased cookie sheet.

3. Bake 8 to 10 minutes or until lightly browned. Cool slightly; remove from cookie sheet to wire rack. Cool completely. *Makes about 5 dozen cookies*

CHOCOLATE COOKIE VARIATION: Add ⅓ cup HERSHEY'S Cocoa to flour mixture.

TIP

Cookies, brownies and bars make great gifts. Place them in a paper-lined tin or on a decorative plate; cover with plastic wrap and tie with a colorful ribbon. For a special touch, include the recipe.

REESE'S® CLASSIC PEANUT BUTTER AND MILK CHOCOLATE CHIP COOKIES

129

CHOCOLATE-ALMOND HONEYS

1¾ cups graham cracker crumbs

1 can (14 ounces) sweetened condensed milk (not evaporated milk)

2 tablespoons honey

2 tablespoons orange or apple juice

1 teaspoon freshly grated orange peel

1 cup HERSHEY'S Semi-Sweet Chocolate Chips

½ cup chopped blanched almonds

1. Heat oven to 350°F. Grease 9-inch square baking pan.

2. Stir together graham cracker crumbs, sweetened condensed milk, honey, orange juice and orange peel in large bowl. Stir in chocolate chips and almonds. Spread batter in prepared pan.

3. Bake 30 minutes or until golden brown. Cool completely in pan on wire rack. Cut into bars.

Makes 20 bars

TIP

For a more fancy appearance, try cutting bar cookies into diamonds. First, cut straight lines 1 or 1½ inches apart the length of the baking pan, then cut straight lines 1½ inches apart diagonally across the pan.

CHOCOLATE-ALMOND HONEYS

HOLIDAY CELEBRATIONS

PECAN MINI KISSES® CUPS

$\frac{1}{2}$ cup (1 stick) butter or margarine, softened
1 package (3 ounces) cream cheese, softened
1 cup all-purpose flour
1 egg
$\frac{2}{3}$ cup packed light brown sugar
1 tablespoon butter, melted
1 teaspoon vanilla extract
Dash salt
72 HERSHEY'S MINI KISSES® Brand Milk Chocolates, divided
$\frac{1}{2}$ to $\frac{3}{4}$ cup coarsely chopped pecans

1. Beat $\frac{1}{2}$ cup softened butter and cream cheese in medium bowl until blended. Add flour; beat well. Cover; refrigerate about 1 hour or until firm enough to handle.

2. Heat oven to 325°F. Stir together egg, brown sugar, 1 tablespoon melted butter, vanilla and salt in small bowl until well blended.

3. Shape chilled dough into 24 balls (1 inch each). Place balls in ungreased small muffin cups ($1\frac{3}{4}$ inches in diameter). Press onto bottoms and up sides of cups. Place 2 chocolate pieces in each cup. Spoon about 1 teaspoon pecans over chocolate. Fill each cup with egg mixture.

4. Bake 25 minutes or until filling is set. Lightly press 1 chocolate into center of each cookie. Cool in pan on wire rack. *Makes 24 cups*

TIP: Use HERSHEY'S Mini Kisses™ Brand Milk Chocolates to decorate cakes, cupcakes, cookies and pies. Stir into slightly softened ice cream or sprinkle over top of a sundae for an added chocolate taste treat.

Prep Time: 25 minutes
Chill Time: 1 hour
Bake Time: 25 minutes
Cool Time: 1 hour

PECAN MINI KISSES® CUPS

HOLIDAY FUDGE TORTE

1 cup all-purpose flour
¾ cup sugar
¼ cup HERSHEY'S Cocoa
1½ teaspoons powdered instant coffee
¾ teaspoon baking soda
¼ teaspoon salt
½ cup (1 stick) butter or margarine, softened
¾ cup dairy sour cream
1 egg
½ teaspoon vanilla extract
Fudge Nut Glaze (recipe follows)

1. Heat oven to 350°F. Grease 9-inch round baking pan; line bottom with wax paper. Grease paper; flour paper and pan.

2. Stir together flour, sugar, cocoa, instant coffee, baking soda and salt in large bowl. Add butter, sour cream, egg and vanilla; beat on low speed of mixer until blended. Increase speed to medium; beat 3 minutes. Pour batter into prepared pan.

3. Bake 30 to 35 minutes or until wooden pick inserted in center comes out clean. Cool 10 minutes. Remove from pan to wire rack; gently peel off wax paper. Cool completely.

4. Prepare Fudge Nut Glaze. Place cake on serving plate; pour glaze evenly over cake, allowing some to run down sides. Refrigerate until glaze is firm, about 1 hour. Cover; refrigerate leftover torte. *Makes 8 to 10 servings*

FUDGE NUT GLAZE

½ cup whipping cream
¼ cup sugar
1 tablespoon butter
1½ teaspoons light corn syrup
⅓ cup HERSHEY'S Semi-Sweet Chocolate Chips
¾ cup chopped MAUNA LOA® Macadamia Nuts, hazelnuts or pecans
½ teaspoon vanilla extract

1. Combine all ingredients except nuts and vanilla in small saucepan. Cook over medium heat, stirring constantly, until mixture boils. Cook, stirring constantly, 5 minutes. Remove from heat.

2. Cool 10 minutes; stir in nuts and vanilla.

HOLIDAY FUDGE TORTE

HOLIDAY DOUBLE PEANUT BUTTER FUDGE COOKIES

1 can (14 ounces) sweetened condensed milk (not evaporated milk)
¾ cup REESE'S® Creamy Peanut Butter
2 cups all-purpose biscuit baking mix
1 teaspoon vanilla extract
¾ cup REESE'S® Peanut Butter Chips
¼ cup granulated sugar
½ teaspoon red colored sugar
½ teaspoon green colored sugar

1. Heat oven to 375°F.

2. Beat sweetened condensed milk and peanut butter with electric mixer on medium speed in large bowl until smooth. Beat in baking mix and vanilla; stir in peanut butter chips. Set aside.

3. Stir together granulated sugar and colored sugars in small bowl. Shape dough into 1-inch balls; roll in sugar. Place 2 inches apart on ungreased cookie sheet; flatten slightly with bottom of glass.

4. Bake 6 to 8 minutes or until very lightly browned (do not overbake). Cool slightly. Remove to wire rack and cool completely. Store in tightly covered container.

Makes about 3½ dozen cookies

TIP

If you're baking several batches of cookies, you can speed things up by placing the cookie dough onto sheets of foil or parchment paper ahead of time. That way they'll be ready to slide right onto cookie sheets and into the oven. Make sure that you let the cookie sheet cool before you bake another batch on the same one or the dough can melt and spread, changing the final shape and texture of the cookies.

HOLIDAY DOUBLE PEANUT BUTTER FUDGE COOKIES

HERSHEY'S CHOCOLATE PEPPERMINT ROLL

CHOCOLATE SPONGE ROLL

4 eggs, separated
$\frac{1}{2}$ cup plus $\frac{1}{3}$ cup granulated sugar, divided
1 teaspoon vanilla extract
$\frac{1}{2}$ cup all-purpose flour
$\frac{1}{3}$ cup HERSHEY'S Cocoa
$\frac{1}{2}$ teaspoon baking powder
$\frac{1}{4}$ teaspoon baking soda
$\frac{1}{8}$ teaspoon salt
$\frac{1}{3}$ cup water

PEPPERMINT FILLING

1 cup cold whipping cream
$\frac{1}{4}$ cup powdered sugar
$\frac{1}{4}$ cup finely crushed hard peppermint candy or $\frac{1}{2}$ teaspoon mint extract
Few drops red food color (optional)

CHOCOLATE GLAZE

2 tablespoons butter or margarine
2 tablespoons HERSHEY'S Cocoa
2 tablespoons water
1 cup powdered sugar
$\frac{1}{2}$ teaspoon vanilla extract

1. For Chocolate Sponge Roll, heat oven to 375°F. Line $15\frac{1}{2} \times 10\frac{1}{2} \times 1$-inch jelly-roll pan with foil; generously grease foil.

2. Beat egg whites with electric mixer on high speed in large bowl until soft peaks form; gradually add $\frac{1}{2}$ cup granulated sugar, beating until stiff peaks form. Set aside.

3. Beat egg yolks and vanilla with electric mixer on medium speed in medium bowl 3 minutes. Gradually add remaining $\frac{1}{3}$ cup granulated sugar; continue beating 2 minutes. Stir together flour, cocoa, baking powder, baking soda and salt. With mixer on low speed, add flour mixture to egg yolk mixture alternately with water, beating just until batter is smooth. Using rubber spatula, gradually fold beaten egg whites into chocolate mixture until well blended. Spread batter evenly in prepared pan.

4. Bake 12 to 15 minutes or until top springs back when touched lightly. Immediately loosen cake from edges of pan; invert onto clean towel sprinkled with powdered sugar. Carefully peel off foil. Immediately roll cake in towel, starting from narrow end; place on wire rack to cool completely.

140

continued on page 142

HERSHEY'S CHOCOLATE PEPPERMINT ROLL

Hershey's Chocolate Peppermint Roll, continued

5. For Peppermint Filling, beat whipping cream with electric mixer on medium speed in medium bowl until slightly thickened. Add $1/4$ cup powdered sugar and peppermint candy or mint extract and food color, if desired; beat cream until stiff peaks form.

6. For Chocolate Glaze, melt butter in small saucepan over very low heat; add cocoa and water, stirring until smooth and slightly thickened. Remove from heat and cool slightly. (Cool completely for thicker frosting.) Gradually beat in 1 cup powdered sugar and vanilla extract.

7. Carefully unroll cake; remove towel. Spread cake with Peppermint Filling; reroll cake. Spread Chocolate Glaze over cake. Refrigerate until just before serving. Cover; refrigerate leftover dessert.

Makes 10 to 12 servings

VARIATION: Substitute Coffee Filling for Peppermint Filling. Combine $1\frac{1}{2}$ cups cold milk and 2 teaspoons instant coffee granules in medium bowl; let stand 5 minutes. Add 1 package (4-serving size) instant vanilla pudding. Beat with electric mixer on lowest speed about 2 minutes or until well blended. Use as directed above to fill Chocolate Sponge Roll.

FOOLPROOF DARK CHOCOLATE FUDGE

3 cups ($1\frac{1}{2}$ packages, 12 ounces each) HERSHEY'S Semi-Sweet Chocolate Chips

1 can (14 ounces) sweetened condensed milk (not evaporated milk)
   Dash salt

1 cup chopped walnuts

$1\frac{1}{2}$ teaspoons vanilla extract

1. Line 8- or 9-inch square pan with foil, extending foil over edges of pan.

2. Melt chocolate chips with sweetened condensed milk and salt in heavy saucepan over low heat. Remove from heat; stir in walnuts and vanilla. Spread evenly into prepared pan.

3. Refrigerate 2 hours or until firm. Remove from pan; place on cutting board. Peel off foil; cut into squares. Store loosely covered at room temperature.

Makes about 5 dozen pieces or 2 pounds

NOTE: For best results, do not double this recipe.

Prep Time: 10 minutes
Cook Time: 15 minutes
Chill Time: 2 hours

CHOCOLATE CHIP PUMPKIN CHEESECAKE

1 cup vanilla wafer crumbs (about 30 wafers, crushed)

¼ cup HERSHEY'S Cocoa

¼ cup powdered sugar

¼ cup (½ stick) butter or margarine, melted

3 packages (8 ounces *each*) cream cheese, softened

1 cup granulated sugar

3 tablespoons all-purpose flour

1 teaspoon pumpkin pie spice

1 cup canned pumpkin

4 eggs

1½ cups HERSHEY'S MINI CHIPS™ Semi-Sweet Chocolate Chips

Chocolate leaves (optional)

1. Heat oven to 350°F.

2. Stir together crumbs, cocoa and powdered sugar in medium bowl; stir in melted butter. Press mixture onto bottom and ½ inch up side of 9-inch springform pan. Bake 8 minutes; cool slightly.

3. *Increase oven temperature to 400°F.*

4. Beat cream cheese, granulated sugar, flour and pumpkin pie spice in large bowl until well blended. Add pumpkin and eggs; beat until well blended. Stir in small chocolate chips; pour batter into prepared crust. Bake 10 minutes.

5. *Reduce oven temperature to 250°F;* continue baking 50 to 60 minutes or until almost set. Remove from oven to wire rack. With knife, loosen cake from side of pan. Cool completely. Refrigerate about 5 hours before serving. Prepare Chocolate Leaves, if desired. Garnish cake with leaves. Cover; refrigerate leftover cheesecake.

Makes 10 to 12 servings

CHOCOLATE LEAVES: Thoroughly wash and dry several non-toxic leaves. Place ½ cup HERSHEY'S MINI CHIPS™ Semi-Sweet Chocolate Chips in small microwave-safe bowl. Microwave at HIGH (100%) 30 to 45 seconds or until smooth when stirred. With small, soft-bristled pastry brush, brush melted chocolate on backs of leaves. (Avoid getting chocolate on leaf front; removal may be difficult when chocolate hardens.) Place on wax paper-covered cookie sheet; refrigerate until very firm. Beginning at stem, carefully pull green leaves from chocolate leaves; refrigerate until ready to use.

TOFFEE BREAD PUDDING WITH CINNAMON TOFFEE SAUCE

3 cups milk

4 eggs

¾ cup sugar

¾ teaspoon ground cinnamon

¾ teaspoon vanilla extract

½ teaspoon salt

6 to 6½ cups ½-inch cubes French, Italian or sourdough bread

1 cup HEATH® BITS 'O BRICKLE® Toffee Bits, divided

Cinnamon Toffee Sauce (recipe follows)

Sweetened whipped cream or ice cream (optional)

1. Heat oven to 350°F. Butter 13×9×2-inch baking pan.

2. Mix together milk, eggs, sugar, cinnamon, vanilla and salt in large bowl with wire whisk. Stir in bread cubes, coating completely. Allow to stand 10 minutes. Stir in ½ cup toffee bits. Pour into prepared pan. Sprinkle remaining ½ cup toffee bits over surface.

3. Bake 40 to 45 minutes or until surface is set. Cool 30 minutes.

4. Meanwhile, prepare Cinnamon Toffee Sauce. Cut pudding into squares; top with sauce and sweetened whipped cream or ice cream, if desired. *Makes 12 servings*

CINNAMON TOFFEE SAUCE: Combine ¾ cup HEATH® BITS 'O BRICKLE® Toffee Bits, ⅓ cup whipping cream and ⅛ teaspoon ground cinnamon in medium saucepan. Cook over low heat, stirring constantly, until toffee melts and mixture is well blended. (As toffee melts, small bits of almond will remain.) Makes about ⅔ cup sauce.

TIP

This dessert is best eaten the same day it is prepared.

TOFFEE BREAD PUDDING WITH CINNAMON TOFFEE SAUCE

HERSHEY'S MINI KISSES® PUMPKIN MOUSSE CUPS

$1\frac{3}{4}$ cups (10-ounce package) HERSHEY'S MINI KISSES® Brand Milk Chocolates, divided

24 marshmallows

$\frac{1}{2}$ cup milk

$\frac{1}{2}$ cup canned pumpkin

1 teaspoon vanilla extract

1 teaspoon pumpkin pie spice

$\frac{1}{3}$ cup powdered sugar

1 cup ($\frac{1}{2}$ pint) cold whipping cream

1. Line 10 muffin cups ($2\frac{1}{2}$ inches in diameter) with paper bake cups. Reserve $\frac{1}{2}$ cup chocolates or chocolate pieces. Place remaining $1\frac{1}{4}$ cups chocolates in small microwave-safe bowl; microwave at HIGH (100%) 1 minute or until melted when stirred. Mixture should be thick.

2. Very thickly coat inside pleated surfaces and bottoms of bake cups with melted chocolate using soft pastry brush. Refrigerate 10 minutes; recoat any thin spots with melted chocolate.* Refrigerate until firm, about 2 hours. Gently peel off paper; refrigerate until ready to fill.

3. Place marshmallows, milk, and pumpkin in medium microwave-safe bowl. Microwave at HIGH 1 minute; stir. Microwave additional 30 seconds at a time, stirring after each heating, until mixture is melted and smooth. Stir in vanilla and pumpkin pie spice. Cool completely.

4. Beat powdered sugar and whipping cream until stiff; fold into pumpkin mixture. Fill cups with pumpkin mousse; garnish with reserved chocolates pieces and additional whipped cream, if desired. Cover; refrigerate 2 hours or until firm.   *Makes 10 servings*

*If reheating is needed, microwave chocolate at HIGH 15 seconds; stir.

HERSHEY'S MINI KISSES® PUMPKIN MOUSSE CUPS

FUDGEY PECAN PIE

⅓ cup butter or margarine

⅔ cup sugar

½ cup HERSHEY'S Cocoa

3 eggs

1 cup light corn syrup

¼ teaspoon salt

1 cup chopped pecans

1 unbaked 9-inch pie crust

Pecan halves (optional)

1. Heat oven to 375°F.

2. Melt butter in medium saucepan over low heat. Add sugar and cocoa; stir until well blended. Remove from heat; cool.

3. Beat eggs slightly in medium bowl. Stir in corn syrup and salt. Add cocoa mixture; blend well. Stir in chopped pecans. Pour into unbaked crust.

4. Bake 45 to 50 minutes or until set. Cool completely on wire rack. Cover; let stand about 8 hours before serving. Garnish pie with pecan halves, if desired.

Makes 8 servings

FUDGEY MOCHA PECAN PIE: Dissolve 1 teaspoon powdered instant coffee in 1 teaspoon hot water in small bowl or cup; add to pie filling when adding corn syrup and salt.

FUDGEY PECAN PIE

CHOCOLATE CAKE SQUARES WITH EGGNOG SAUCE

1½ teaspoons baking soda
1 cup buttermilk or sour milk*
¾ cup HERSHEY'S Cocoa
¾ cup boiling water
¼ cup (½ stick) butter or margarine, softened
¼ cup shortening
2 cups sugar
2 eggs
1 teaspoon vanilla extract
⅛ teaspoon salt
1¾ cups all-purpose flour
Eggnog Sauce (recipe follows)

*To sour milk: Use 1 tablespoon white vinegar plus milk to equal 1 cup.

1. Heat oven to 350°F. Grease and flour 13×9×2-inch baking pan.

2. Stir baking soda into buttermilk in medium bowl; set aside. Stir together cocoa and water until smooth; set aside.

3. Beat butter, shortening and sugar in large bowl until creamy. Add eggs, vanilla and salt; beat well. Add buttermilk mixture alternately with flour to butter mixture, beating until blended. Add cocoa mixture; blend thoroughly. Pour batter into prepared pan.

4. Bake 40 to 45 minutes or until wooden pick inserted in center comes out clean. Cool completely. Prepare Eggnog Sauce. Serve cake with sauce.   *Makes 12 to 15 servings*

EGGNOG SAUCE

1 tablespoon cornstarch
2 tablespoons cold water
1⅓ cups milk
¼ cup sugar
3 egg yolks, beaten
¼ teaspoon *each* brandy and vanilla extracts
Several dashes ground nutmeg

Stir cornstarch and water in saucepan until smooth. Add milk, sugar and egg yolks. Beat with whisk until well blended. Cook over medium heat, stirring constantly, until thickened. Remove from heat. Stir in extracts. Cool completely. Sprinkle nutmeg over top. Cover; refrigerate leftover sauce.   *Makes about 1¾ cups sauce*

CHOCOLATE CAKE SQUARE WITH EGGNOG SAUCE

CHOCOLATE SNOWBALL COOKIES

1 cup (2 sticks) butter or margarine, softened
¾ cup packed light brown sugar
1 egg
1 teaspoon vanilla extract
2 cups all-purpose flour
½ cup HERSHEY'S SPECIAL DARK® Cocoa or HERSHEY'S Cocoa
1 teaspoon baking powder
¼ teaspoon baking soda
3 tablespoons milk
¾ cup finely chopped macadamia nuts or almonds
¾ cup HEATH® BITS 'O BRICKLE® Toffee Bits
Powdered sugar

1. Beat butter, brown sugar, egg and vanilla in large bowl until blended. Stir together flour, cocoa, baking powder and baking soda; add with milk to butter mixture until well blended. Stir in nuts and toffee.

2. Refrigerate until firm enough to handle, at least 2 hours. Heat oven to 350°F. Shape dough into 1-inch balls; place 2 inches apart on ungreased cookie sheet.

3. Bake 8 to 10 minutes or until set. Remove from cookie sheet to wire rack. Cool completely; roll in powdered sugar. *Makes about 4 dozen cookies*

DECADENT HOLIDAY CHOCOLATE TORTE

    3 eggs, separated
 $\frac{1}{8}$ teaspoon cream of tartar
 $1\frac{1}{2}$ cups sugar
    1 cup (2 sticks) butter or margarine, melted
    2 teaspoons vanilla extract
 $\frac{1}{2}$ cup all-purpose flour
 $\frac{1}{2}$ cup HERSHEY'S Cocoa or HERSHEY'S SPECIAL DARK® Cocoa
 $\frac{1}{4}$ cup water
    1 cup finely chopped pecans
    Semi-Sweet Glaze (recipe follows)
    Snowy White Cut-Outs (recipe follows, optional)

1. Heat oven to 350°F. Line bottom and sides of 9-inch springform pan with foil; grease foil.

2. Beat egg whites and cream of tartar in small bowl until soft peaks form; set aside. Beat egg yolks, sugar, melted butter and vanilla in large bowl until well blended. Add flour, cocoa and water; stir in pecans. Gradually fold reserved egg white mixture into chocolate mixture; spread into prepared pan.

3. Bake 45 to 55 minutes or until firm to touch; cool completely in pan on wire rack. Invert onto serving plate; remove foil. Cover; refrigerate. Prepare Semi-Sweet Glaze. Spread top and sides of torte with prepared glaze. Cover; refrigerate. Prepare Snowy White Cut-Outs, if desired; garnish top of torte with cut-outs. *Makes 12 servings*

SEMI-SWEET GLAZE: Place 1 cup HERSHEY'S Semi-Sweet Chocolate Chips and $\frac{1}{3}$ cup whipping cream in small microwave-safe bowl. Microwave at HIGH (100%) 1 minute; stir until smooth. Use immediately.

SNOWY WHITE CUT-OUTS: Line tray with heavy duty foil. Melt 2 cups (12-ounce package) HERSHEY'S Premier White Chips and 1 teaspoon shortening (do *not* use butter, margarine, spread or oil) as directed on package. Immediately spread mixture about $\frac{1}{8}$ inch thick on prepared tray. Before mixture is firm, cut into desired shapes with small cookie cutters; do not remove from tray. Cover; refrigerate until firm. Gently peel off shapes.

FESTIVE FUDGE

3 cups (1½ packages, 12 ounces *each*) HERSHEY'S Semi-Sweet Chocolate
Chips
1 can (14 ounces) sweetened condensed milk (not evaporated milk)
Dash salt
½ to 1 cup chopped nuts (optional)
1½ teaspoons vanilla extract

1. Line 8- or 9-inch square pan with wax paper.

2. Melt chocolate chips with sweetened condensed milk and salt in heavy saucepan over low heat. Remove from heat; stir in nuts, if desired, and vanilla. Spread evenly into prepared pan.

3. Refrigerate 2 hours or until firm. Turn fudge onto cutting board; peel off paper and cut into squares. Store covered in refrigerator. *Makes about 2 pounds*

CHOCOLATE PEANUT BUTTER CHIP GLAZED FUDGE: Proceed as above; stir in ⅔ cup REESE'S® Peanut Butter Chips in place of nuts. Melt 1 cup REESE'S® Peanut Butter Chips with ½ cup whipping cream; stir until thick and smooth. Spread over fudge.

TIP

If fudge is difficult to cut into neat squares,
place it in the refrigerator or freezer until firm.
This will make it easier to cut.

CHOCOLATE PEANUT BUTTER CHIP GLAZED FUDGE

BUCHE DE NOEL COOKIES

2/3 cup butter or margarine, softened
1 cup granulated sugar
2 eggs
2 teaspoons vanilla extract
2½ cups all-purpose flour
½ cup HERSHEY'S Cocoa
½ teaspoon baking soda
¼ teaspoon salt
Mocha Frosting (recipe follows)
Powdered sugar (optional)

1. Beat butter and sugar with electric mixer on medium speed in large bowl until well blended. Add eggs and vanilla; beat until fluffy. Stir together flour, cocoa, baking soda and salt; gradually add to butter mixture, beating until well blended. Cover; refrigerate dough 1 to 2 hours.

2. Heat oven to 350°F. Shape heaping teaspoons of dough into logs about 2½ inches long and ¾ inches in diameter; place on ungreased cookie sheet. Bake 7 to 9 minutes or until set. Cool slightly. Remove to wire rack and cool completely. Prepare Mocha Frosting.

3. Frost cookies with frosting. Using tines of fork, draw lines through frosting to imitate tree bark. Lightly dust with powdered sugar, if desired. *Makes about 2½ dozen cookies*

MOCHA FROSTING

6 tablespoons butter or margarine, softened
2⅔ cups powdered sugar
⅓ cup HERSHEY'S Cocoa
3 to 4 tablespoons milk
2 teaspoons powdered instant espresso dissolved in 1 teaspoon hot water
1 teaspoon vanilla extract

Beat butter with electric mixer on medium speed in medium bowl until creamy. Add powdered sugar and cocoa alternately with milk, dissolved espresso and vanilla, beating to spreadable consistency. *Makes about 1⅔ cups frosting*

BUCHE DE NOEL COOKIES

HOLIDAY COCONUT CAKE

COCONUT CAKE

$\frac{1}{2}$ cup (1 stick) butter or margarine, softened

$\frac{1}{2}$ cup shortening

2 cups sugar

5 eggs, separated

1 teaspoon vanilla extract

2 cups all-purpose flour

1 teaspoon baking soda

$\frac{1}{4}$ teaspoon salt

1 cup buttermilk

2 cups MOUNDS® Sweetened Coconut Flakes

$\frac{1}{2}$ cup chopped pecans

TOFFEE CREAM

2 cups cold whipping cream

$\frac{1}{4}$ cup powdered sugar

1 teaspoon vanilla extract

$\frac{1}{2}$ cup HEATH® BITS 'O BRICKLE® Toffee Bits

Additional HEATH® BITS 'O BRICKLE® Toffee Bits (optional)

1. Heat oven to 350°F. Grease and flour 12-cup fluted tube pan.

2. Beat butter, shortening, sugar, egg yolks and vanilla with electric mixer on medium speed in large bowl until creamy. Stir together flour, baking soda and salt; add alternately with buttermilk, beating until well blended. Stir in coconut and pecans.

3. Beat egg whites with electric mixer on high speed in large bowl until stiff peaks form; fold into batter. Pour batter into prepared pan.

4. Bake 45 to 55 minutes or until wooden pick inserted in center comes out clean. Cool 10 minutes; remove from pan to wire rack. Cool completely.

5. For Toffee Cream, beat whipping cream, powdered sugar and vanilla extract with electric mixer on medium speed in large bowl until stiff peaks form. Fold in toffee bits. Frost cake with Toffee Cream. Garnish with additional toffee bits, if desired. Cover; store leftover cake in refrigerator. *Makes 12 servings*

HOLIDAY COCONUT CAKE

CHOCOLATE MINI-PUFFS

$\frac{1}{2}$ cup water
$\frac{1}{4}$ cup ($\frac{1}{2}$ stick) butter or margarine
$\frac{1}{8}$ teaspoon salt
$\frac{1}{2}$ cup all-purpose flour
2 eggs
Chocolate Mousse Filling (recipe follows)
Chocolate Glaze (page 162) or powdered sugar

1. Heat oven to 400°F.

2. Combine water, butter and salt in medium saucepan. Cook over medium heat, stirring constantly, until mixture comes to full rolling boil; turn heat to low.

3. Add flour all at once; cook over low heat, stirring vigorously, until mixture leaves side of pan and forms a ball, about 1 minute. Remove from heat; cool slightly. Add eggs, one at a time, beating with wooden spoon until smooth and velvety. Drop by scant teaspoonfuls onto ungreased cookie sheet.

4. Bake 25 to 30 minutes or until puffed and golden brown. Remove from oven; cool on wire rack.

5. Prepare Chocolate Mousse Filling. Slice off tops of puffs. With spoon, fill puffs with filling or pipe filling into puffs using a pastry bag fitted with $\frac{1}{4}$-inch tip. Replace tops. Prepare Chocolate Glaze; drizzle onto puffs. Refrigerate until serving time. Cover; refrigerate leftover puffs.

Makes about 2 to 2$\frac{1}{2}$ dozen mini-puffs

CHOCOLATE MOUSSE FILLING

1 teaspoon unflavored gelatin
1 tablespoon cold water
2 tablespoons boiling water
$\frac{1}{2}$ cup sugar
$\frac{1}{4}$ cup HERSHEY'S Cocoa
1 cup ($\frac{1}{2}$ pint) cold whipping cream
1 teaspoon vanilla extract

1. Sprinkle gelatin over cold water in small bowl; let stand 1 minute to soften. Add boiling water; stir until gelatin is completely dissolved and mixture is clear. Cool slightly.

2. Stir together sugar and cocoa in medium bowl; add whipping cream and vanilla. Beat at medium speed, scraping bottom of bowl occasionally, until stiff; pour in gelatin mixture and beat until well blended. Refrigerate $\frac{1}{2}$ hour. *Makes about 2 cups filling*

continued on page 162

CHOCOLATE MINI-PUFFS

Chocolate Mini-Puffs, continued

CHOCOLATE GLAZE: Melt 2 tablespoons butter or margarine in small saucepan over low heat; add 2 tablespoons HERSHEY'S Cocoa and 2 tablespoons water. Cook and stir over low heat until smooth and slightly thickened; do not boil. Remove from heat; cool slightly. Gradually add in 1 cup powdered sugar and $\frac{1}{2}$ teaspoon vanilla extract, beating to desired consistency. Makes about $\frac{3}{4}$ cup glaze.

WINTER WONDERLAND SNOWMEN BROWNIES

$\frac{3}{4}$ cup HERSHEY'S Cocoa or HERSHEY'S SPECIAL DARK® Cocoa
$\frac{1}{2}$ teaspoon baking soda
$\frac{2}{3}$ cup butter or margarine, melted and divided
$\frac{1}{2}$ cup boiling water
2 cups sugar
2 eggs
1 teaspoon vanilla extract
$1\frac{1}{2}$ cups all-purpose flour
$1\frac{2}{3}$ cups (10-ounce package) REESE'S® Peanut Butter Chips
    Powdered sugar (optional)

1. Heat oven to 350°F. Line 13×9×2-inch baking pan with foil; grease foil.

2. Stir together cocoa and baking soda in large bowl; stir in $\frac{1}{3}$ cup melted butter. Add boiling water; stir until mixture thickens. Stir in sugar, eggs, vanilla and remaining $\frac{1}{3}$ cup butter; stir until smooth. Add flour; stir until blended. Stir in peanut butter chips. Pour into prepared pan.

3. Bake 35 to 40 minutes or until brownies begin to pull away from sides of foil. Cool completely in pan. Cover; refrigerate until firm. Remove from pan; remove foil. Cut into snowmen shapes with cookie cutters or cut into squares. Just before serving, sprinkle with powdered sugar, if desired.   *Makes about 12 large brownies or 36 squares*

CANDY-KISSED TWISTS

36 HERSHEY'S KISSES® Brand Milk Chocolates
1 bag small pretzels (twisted)
Decorative garnishes such as: REESE'S® PIECES® Candies, silver dragées, small holiday themed candies, nut pieces, miniature marshmallows, candied cherry pieces

1. Heat oven to 350°F. Remove wrappers from chocolates.

2. Place pretzels on ungreased cookie sheet. Place a chocolate on top of each pretzel.

3. Bake 2 to 3 minutes or until the chocolate is soft, but not melting.

4. Remove from oven; gently press decorative garnish on top of softened chocolate piece. Cool.

Makes about 36 pieces

PEANUT BUTTER CHIP BRITTLE

1⅔ cups (10-ounce package) REESE'S® Peanut Butter Chips, divided
1½ cups (3 sticks) butter or margarine
1¾ cups sugar
3 tablespoons light corn syrup
3 tablespoons water

1. Butter 15½×10½×1-inch jelly-roll pan.* Sprinkle 1 cup peanut butter chips evenly onto bottom of prepared pan; set aside.

2. Melt butter in heavy 2½-quart saucepan. Add sugar, corn syrup and water. Stir constantly over medium heat until mixture reaches 300°F on candy thermometer. (Bulb of thermometer should not rest on bottom of saucepan.) Remove from heat. Immediately spread mixture into prepared pan; sprinkle with remaining ⅔ cup peanut butter chips. Cool completely.

3. Remove from pan. Break into pieces. Store in tightly covered container in cool, dry place.

Makes about 2 pounds brittle

For thicker brittle, use a 13×9×2-inch pan.

NOTE: For best results, do *not* double this recipe.

163

HOLIDAY RED RASPBERRY CHOCOLATE BARS

$2\frac{1}{2}$ cups all-purpose flour
1 cup sugar
$\frac{3}{4}$ cup finely chopped pecans
1 egg, beaten
1 cup (2 sticks) cold butter or margarine
1 jar (12 ounces) seedless red raspberry jam
$1\frac{2}{3}$ cups HERSHEY'S Milk Chocolate Chips, HERSHEY'S Semi-Sweet Chocolate Chips or HERSHEY'S MINI KISSES® Brand Milk Chocolates

1. Heat oven to 350°F. Grease 13×9×2-inch baking pan.

2. Stir together flour, sugar, pecans and egg in large bowl. Cut in butter with pastry blender or fork until mixture resembles coarse crumbs; set aside $1\frac{1}{2}$ cups crumb mixture. Press remaining crumb mixture on bottom of prepared pan. Stir jam to soften; carefully spread over crumb mixture in pan. Sprinkle with chocolate chips. Crumble reserved crumb mixture evenly over top.

3. Bake 40 to 45 minutes or until lightly browned. Cool completely in pan on wire rack; cut into bars.

Makes 36 bars

TIP

Cookies, brownies and bars make great gifts.
Place them in a paper-lined tin or on a decorative
plate; cover with plastic wrap and tie with a colorful
ribbon. For a special touch, include the recipe.

HOLIDAY RED RASPBERRY CHOCOLATE BARS

GLAZED CRANBERRY MINI-CAKES

$\frac{1}{3}$ cup butter or margarine, softened

$\frac{1}{3}$ cup granulated sugar

$\frac{1}{3}$ cup packed light brown sugar

1 egg

$1\frac{1}{4}$ teaspoons vanilla extract

$1\frac{1}{3}$ cups all-purpose flour

$\frac{3}{4}$ teaspoon baking powder

$\frac{1}{4}$ teaspoon baking soda

$\frac{1}{4}$ teaspoon salt

2 tablespoons milk

$1\frac{1}{4}$ cups coarsely chopped fresh cranberries

$\frac{1}{2}$ cup coarsely chopped walnuts

$1\frac{2}{3}$ cups HERSHEY'S Premier White Chips, divided

White Glaze (recipe follows)

1. Heat oven to 350°F. Lightly grease or paper-line 36 small muffin cups ($1\frac{3}{4}$ inches in diameter).

2. Beat butter, granulated sugar, brown sugar, egg and vanilla in large bowl until fluffy. Stir together flour, baking powder, baking soda and salt; gradually blend into butter mixture. Add milk; stir until blended. Stir in cranberries, walnuts and $\frac{2}{3}$ cup white chips (reserve remaining chips for glaze). Fill muffin cups almost full with batter.

3. Bake 18 to 20 minutes or until wooden pick inserted in center comes out clean. Cool 5 minutes; remove from pans to wire rack. Cool completely. Prepare White Glaze; drizzle over top of mini-cakes. Refrigerate 10 minutes to set glaze.

Makes about 3 dozen mini-cakes

WHITE GLAZE: Place remaining 1 cup HERSHEY'S Premier White Chips in small microwave-safe bowl; sprinkle 2 tablespoons vegetable oil over chips. Microwave at HIGH (100% power) 30 seconds; stir. If necessary, microwave at HIGH additional 30 seconds or just until chips are melted when stirred.

GLAZED CRANBERRY MINI-CAKES

COLORFUL KWANZAA BROWNIES

$\frac{3}{4}$ cup ($1\frac{1}{2}$ sticks) butter or margarine, melted

$1\frac{1}{2}$ cups sugar

$1\frac{1}{2}$ teaspoons vanilla extract

3 eggs

$\frac{3}{4}$ cup all-purpose flour

$\frac{1}{2}$ cup HERSHEY'S Cocoa

$\frac{1}{2}$ teaspoon baking powder

$\frac{1}{4}$ teaspoon salt

$\frac{2}{3}$ cup chopped pecans (optional)

Chocolate Cream (recipe follows)

Assorted fresh fruit, sliced or cut up (banana, mango, papaya, peaches, pineapple or strawberries)

1. Heat oven to 350°F. Grease 12-inch round pizza pan or 13×9×2-inch baking pan.

2. Combine butter, sugar and vanilla in large bowl. Add eggs; beat well with spoon. Combine flour, cocoa, baking powder and salt; gradually stir into egg mixture until blended. Stir in pecans, if desired. Spread batter into prepared pan.

3. Bake 20 to 22 minutes or until top springs back when touched lightly in center. Cool completely. Prepare Chocolate Cream. Spread cream over top. Refrigerate about 30 minutes. Garnish with fruit just before serving. Store covered in refrigerator without fruit topping.

Makes 12 to 15 servings

CHOCOLATE CREAM

1 package (8 ounces) cream cheese, softened

$\frac{1}{2}$ cup sugar

3 tablespoons HERSHEY'S Cocoa

1 tablespoon milk

$1\frac{1}{2}$ teaspoons vanilla extract

Beat all ingredients in bowl until smooth.

Makes about 1 cup cream

COLORFUL KWANZAA BROWNIES

HOLIDAY CHOCOLATE CAKE

2 cups sugar

1¾ cups all-purpose flour

¾ cup HERSHEY'S Cocoa

2 teaspoons baking soda

1 teaspoon baking powder

1 teaspoon salt

1 cup buttermilk or sour milk*

1 cup strong black coffee *or* 2 teaspoons instant coffee dissolved in 1 cup hot water

½ cup vegetable oil

2 eggs

2 teaspoons vanilla extract

Ricotta Cheese Filling (page 172)

Chocolate Whipped Cream (recipe follows)

Vanilla Whipped Cream (recipe follows)

Candied red or green cherries (optional)

To sour milk: Use 1 tablespoon white vinegar plus milk to equal 1 cup.

1. Heat oven to 350°F. Grease and flour two 9-inch round baking pans.

2. Stir together sugar, flour, cocoa, baking soda, baking powder and salt in large bowl. Add buttermilk, coffee, oil, eggs and vanilla; beat at medium speed of mixer 2 minutes (batter will be thin). Pour batter into prepared pans.

3. Bake 30 to 35 minutes or until wooden pick inserted into centers of cakes comes out clean. Cool 10 minutes; remove from pans to wire racks. Cool completely. Prepare Ricotta Cheese Filling.

4. Slice cake layers in half horizontally. Place bottom slice on serving plate; top with ⅓ Ricotta Cheese Filling. Alternate cake layers and filling, ending with cake on top. Prepare whipped creams. Frost cake with Chocolate Whipped Cream. Decorate with Vanilla Whipped Cream and cherries, if desired. Cover; refrigerate leftover cake.

Makes 10 to 12 servings

CHOCOLATE WHIPPED CREAM: Stir together ⅓ cup powdered sugar and 2 tablespoons HERSHEY'S Cocoa in small bowl. Add 1 cup (½ pint) cold whipping cream and 1 teaspoon vanilla extract; beat until stiff.

VANILLA WHIPPED CREAM: Beat ½ cup cold whipping cream, 2 tablespoons powdered sugar and ½ teaspoon vanilla extract in small bowl until stiff.

continued on page 172

HOLIDAY CHOCOLATE CAKE

Holiday Chocolate Cake, continued

RICOTTA CHEESE FILLING

1¾ cups (15 ounces) ricotta cheese*
¼ cup sugar
3 tablespoons Grand Marnier (orange-flavored liqueur) or orange juice concentrate, undiluted
¼ cup candied red or green cherries, coarsely chopped
⅓ cup HERSHEY'S MINI CHIPS™ Semi-Sweet Chocolate Chips

1 cup (½ pint) whipping cream can be substituted for ricotta cheese. Beat with sugar and liqueur until stiff. Fold in candied cherries and small chocolate chips.

Beat ricotta cheese, sugar and liqueur in large bowl until smooth. Fold in candied cherries and small chocolate chips.

CHOCOLATE & CREAMY ORANGE MOUSSE

¼ cup (½ stick) butter or margarine
¼ cup HERSHEY'S Cocoa
1 can (14 ounces) sweetened condensed milk (not evaporated milk), divided
2 tablespoons orange juice plus 2 teaspoons freshly grated orange peel *or* 2 tablespoons orange-flavored liqueur, divided
2 cups (1 pint) cold whipping cream

1. Melt butter in heavy saucepan over low heat; add cocoa, then ⅔ cup sweetened condensed milk, stirring until smooth and slightly thickened. Pour mixture into medium bowl; cool to room temperature. Beat in 1 tablespoon orange juice and 1 teaspoon orange peel.

2. Beat whipping cream in large bowl until stiff. Fold half of whipped cream into chocolate mixture. In second medium bowl, stir together remaining sweetened condensed milk, remaining 1 tablespoon orange juice and 1 teaspoon orange peel. Fold in remaining whipped cream.

3. Spoon equal portions of chocolate mixture into 8 dessert dishes, making a depression in center of each. Spoon creamy orange mixture into center of each. Refrigerate until well chilled. Garnish as desired. Cover; refrigerate leftover dessert.

Makes 8 servings

HOLIDAY TREASURE COOKIES

1$\frac{1}{2}$ cups graham cracker crumbs
$\frac{1}{2}$ cup all-purpose flour
2 teaspoons baking powder
1 can (14 ounces) sweetened condensed milk (not evaporated milk)
$\frac{1}{2}$ cup (1 stick) butter, softened
1$\frac{3}{4}$ cups (10-ounce package) HERSHEY'S MINI KISSES® Brand Milk Chocolates
1$\frac{1}{3}$ cups candy coated chocolate pieces
1$\frac{1}{3}$ cups MOUNDS® Sweetened Coconut Flakes
1 cup coarsely chopped walnuts

1. Heat oven to 375°F. Stir together graham cracker crumbs, flour and baking powder in small bowl; set aside.

2. Beat sweetened condensed milk and butter until smooth; add reserved crumb mixture, mixing well. Stir in chocolate pieces, candy coated chocolate pieces, coconut and walnuts. Drop by rounded tablespoons onto ungreased cookie sheet.

3. Bake 8 to 10 minutes or until lightly browned. Cool 1 minute; remove from cookie sheet to wire rack. Cool completely. *Makes about 3 dozen cookies*

COCOA NUT BUNDLES

1 can (8 ounces) refrigerated quick crescent dinner rolls
2 tablespoons butter or margarine, softened
1 tablespoon granulated sugar
2 teaspoons HERSHEY'S Cocoa
$\frac{1}{4}$ cup chopped nuts
Powdered sugar (optional)

1. Heat oven to 375°F. Unroll dough on ungreased cookie sheet and separate to form 8 triangles.

2. Combine butter, granulated sugar and cocoa in small bowl. Add nuts; mix thoroughly. Divide chocolate mixture evenly among the triangles, placing on wide end of triangle. Take dough on either side of mixture and pull up and over mixture, tucking ends under. Continue rolling dough toward the opposite point.

3. Bake 9 to 10 minutes or until golden brown. Sprinkle with powdered sugar, if desired; serve warm. *Makes 8 rolls*

BAKED APPLE SLICES WITH PEANUT BUTTER CRUMBLE

4 cups peeled and thinly sliced apples
1 cup sugar, divided
1 cup all-purpose flour, divided
3 tablespoons butter or margarine, divided
1 cup quick-cooking or old-fashioned rolled oats
½ teaspoon ground cinnamon
1 cup REESE'S® Creamy or Crunchy Peanut Butter
Sweetened whipped cream or ice cream (optional)

1. Heat oven to 350°F. Grease 9-inch square baking pan.

2. Stir together apples, ¾ cup sugar and ¼ cup flour in large bowl. Spread in prepared pan; dot with 2 tablespoons butter. Combine oats, remaining ¾ cup flour, remaining ¼ cup sugar and cinnamon in medium bowl; set aside.

3. Place remaining 1 tablespoon butter and peanut butter in small microwave-safe bowl. Microwave at HIGH (100%) 30 seconds or until butter is melted; stir until smooth. Add to oat mixture; blend until crumbs are formed. Sprinkle crumb mixture over apples.

4. Bake 40 to 45 minutes or until apples are tender and edges are bubbly. Cool slightly. Serve warm or cool with whipped cream or ice cream, if desired.

Makes 6 to 8 servings

TIP

Try using Granny Smith, Jonathan or Golden Delicious apples in this delicious crumble.

BAKED APPLE SLICES WITH PEANUT BUTTER CRUMBLE

CHOCOLATE RASPBERRY DESSERT

1 cup all-purpose flour

1 cup sugar

$\frac{1}{2}$ cup (1 stick) butter or margarine, softened

$\frac{1}{4}$ teaspoon baking powder

4 eggs

$1\frac{1}{2}$ cups (16-ounce can) HERSHEY'S Syrup

Raspberry Cream Center (recipe follows)

Chocolate Glaze (recipe follows)

1. Heat oven to 350°F. Grease 13×9×2-inch baking pan.

2. Combine flour, sugar, butter, baking powder and eggs in large bowl; beat until smooth. Add syrup; blend thoroughly. Pour batter into prepared pan.

3. Bake 25 to 30 minutes or until wooden pick inserted in center comes out clean. Cool completely in pan on wire rack. Prepare Rasberry Cream Center and Chocolate Glaze. Spread cream center on cake. Cover; refrigerate. Pour glaze over chilled dessert. Cover; refrigerate at least 1 hour before serving. Cover; refrigerate leftover dessert.

Makes about 12 servings

RASPBERRY CREAM CENTER: Combine 2 cups powdered sugar, $\frac{1}{2}$ cup (1 stick) softened butter or margarine and 2 tablespoons raspberry-flavored liqueur* in small bowl; beat until smooth. (A few drops red food coloring may be added, if desired.) *$\frac{1}{4}$ cup raspberry preserves and 1 teaspoon water may be substituted for the raspberry-flavored liqueur.

CHOCOLATE GLAZE: Melt 6 tablespoons butter or margarine and 1 cup HERSHEY'S Semi-Sweet Chocolate Chips in small saucepan over very low heat. Remove from heat; stir until smooth. Cool slightly.

DOUBLE RASPBERRY CHOCOLATE DESSERT: Substitute 1 cup HERSHEY'S Raspberry Chips for Semi-Sweet Chocolate Chips in the Chocolate Glaze.

CHOCOLATE RASPBERRY DESSERT

FIRESIDE STEAMED PUDDING

1½ cups plain dry bread crumbs
1 cup sugar, divided
2 tablespoons all-purpose flour
½ teaspoon baking powder
⅛ teaspoon salt
6 eggs, separated
1 can (21 ounces) cherry pie filling, divided
2 tablespoons butter or margarine, melted
½ teaspoon almond extract
¼ teaspoon red food color
1 cup HERSHEY'S MINI CHIPS™ Semi-Sweet Chocolate Chips
Cherry Whipped Cream (recipe follows)

1. Thoroughly grease 8-cup tube mold or heat-proof bowl.

2. Stir together bread crumbs, ¾ cup sugar, flour, baking powder and salt in large bowl. Stir together egg yolks, 1½ cups cherry pie filling, butter, almond extract and food color in medium bowl; add to crumb mixture, stirring gently until well blended.

3. Beat egg whites in another large bowl until foamy; gradually add remaining ¼ cup sugar, beating until stiff peaks form. Fold about ⅓ beaten whites into cherry mixture, blending thoroughly. Fold in remaining egg whites; gently fold in small chocolate chips. Pour batter into prepared tube mold. (If mold is open at top, cover opening with foil; grease top of foil.) Cover mold with wax paper and foil; tie securely with string.

4. Place a rack in large kettle; pour water into kettle to top of rack. Heat water to boiling; place mold on rack. Cover kettle; steam over simmering water about 1½ hours or until wooden pick inserted comes out clean. (Additional water may be needed during steaming.) Remove from heat; cool in pan 5 minutes. Remove cover; unmold onto serving plate. Prepare Cherry Whipped Cream. Serve pudding warm with whipped cream.
Makes 12 to 14 servings

CHERRY WHIPPED CREAM: Beat 1 cup (½ pint) cold whipping cream with ¼ cup powdered sugar in medium bowl until stiff; fold in pie filling remaining from pudding (about ½ cup) and ½ teaspoon almond extract.

FIRESIDE STEAMED PUDDING

NO-BAKE DESSERTS

CHOCOLATE DREAM CUPS

1 cup HERSHEY'S Semi-Sweet Chocolate Chips
1 teaspoon shortening (do *not* use butter, margarine, spread or oil)
    Chocolate Filling or Raspberry Filling (page 184)

1. Line 6 muffin cups (2½ inches in diameter) with paper cup liners.

2. Place chocolate chips and shortening in small microwave-safe bowl. Microwave at HIGH (100%) 1 minute; stir. If necessary, microwave at HIGH 30 seconds or until chips are melted and mixture is smooth when stirred.

3. Coat inside pleated surface and bottoms of cup liners thickly and evenly with melted chocolate using a soft-bristled pastry brush. Refrigerate coated cups 10 minutes or until set; recoat any thin spots with melted chocolate. (If necessary, chocolate can be reheated on HIGH for a few seconds.) Refrigerate cups until very firm, 2 hours or overnight. Carefully peel paper from each chocolate cup. Cover; refrigerate until ready to use.

4. Prepare either Chocolate or Raspberry Filling. Spoon or pipe into chocolate cups; refrigerate until set. Garnish as desired. *Makes 6 dessert cups*

CHOCOLATE FILLING

1 teaspoon unflavored gelatin
1 tablespoon cold water
2 tablespoons boiling water
½ cup sugar
¼ cup HERSHEY'S Cocoa
1 cup (8 ounces) cold whipping cream
1 teaspoon vanilla extract

1. Sprinkle gelatin over cold water in small bowl; let stand 1 minute to soften. Add boiling water; stir until gelatin is completely dissolved and mixture is clear. Cool slightly.

2. Stir together sugar and cocoa in another small bowl; add whipping cream and vanilla. Beat on medium speed, scraping bottom of bowl occasionally until stiff. Pour in gelatin mixture; beat until well blended.

continued on page 184

CHOCOLATE DREAM CUPS

Chocolate Dream Cups, continued

RASPBERRY FILLING

    1 package (10 ounces) frozen red raspberries, thawed
    1 teaspoon unflavored gelatin
    1 tablespoon cold water
    2 tablespoons boiling water
    1 cup (8 ounces) cold whipping cream
    ¼ cup powdered sugar
    ½ teaspoon vanilla extract
    3 to 4 drops red food coloring

1. Drain raspberries; press berries through sieve to remove seeds. Discard seeds.

2. Sprinkle gelatin over cold water in small bowl; let stand 1 minute to soften. Add boiling water; stir until gelatin is completely dissolved and mixture is clear. Cool slightly.

3. Beat whipping cream and sugar in another small bowl until soft peaks form; pour in gelatin mixture and beat until stiff. Carefully fold in raspberry purée and food coloring; refrigerate 20 minutes.

EASY CHOCOBERRY CREAM DESSERT

    2 packages (3 ounces *each*) ladyfingers, split
    1 package (10 ounces) frozen strawberries in syrup, thawed and drained
    2 envelopes unflavored gelatin
    2 cups milk, divided
    1 cup sugar
    ⅓ cup HERSHEY:S Cocoa or HERSHEY:S Special Dark® Cocoa
    ¼ cup (½ stick) butter or margarine
    1 teaspoon vanilla extract
    2 cups frozen non-dairy whipped topping, thawed

1. Place ladyfingers, cut side in, on bottom and around sides of 9-inch springform pan.

2. Purée strawberries in food processor. Sprinkle gelatin over 1 cup milk in medium saucepan; let stand 2 minutes to soften. Add sugar, cocoa and butter. Cook over medium heat, stirring constantly, until mixture is hot and gelatin is completely dissolved. Remove from heat; stir in remaining 1 cup milk, vanilla and puréed strawberries. Refrigerate until mixture begins to thicken.

3. Fold 2 cups whipped topping into gelatin mixture. Pour mixture into prepared pan. Cover; refrigerate until mixture is firm. Just before serving, remove side of pan. Garnish as desired. Cover; refrigerate leftover dessert. *Makes 10 to 12 servings*

EASY CHOCOBERRY CREAM DESSERT

CHOCOLATE-COVERED BANANA POPS

3 ripe large bananas
9 wooden popsicle sticks
2 cups (12-ounce package) HERSHEY'S Semi-Sweet Chocolate Chips
2 tablespoons shortening (do *not* use butter, margarine, spread or oil)
1½ cups coarsely chopped unsalted, roasted peanuts

1. Peel bananas; cut each into thirds. Insert a wooden stick into each banana piece; place on wax paper-covered tray. Cover; freeze until firm.

2. Place chocolate chips and shortening in medium microwave-safe bowl. Microwave at HIGH (100%) 1½ to 2 minutes or until chocolate is melted and mixture is smooth when stirred.

3. Remove bananas from freezer just before dipping. Dip each piece into warm chocolate, covering completely; allow excess to drip off. Immediately roll in peanuts. Cover; return to freezer. Serve frozen.

Makes 9 pops

VARIATION: HERSHEY'S Milk Chocolate Chips or HERSHEY'S MINI CHIPS® Semi-Sweet Chocolate Chips may be substituted for HERSHEY'S Semi-Sweet Chocolate Chips.

SPECIAL DARK® FUDGE TRUFFLES

2 cups (12-ounce package) HERSHEY'S SPECIAL DARK® Chocolate Chips
¾ cup whipping cream
Various coatings such as toasted chopped pecans, coconut, powdered sugar, cocoa or small candy pieces

1. Combine chocolate chips and cream in medium microwave-safe bowl. Microwave at HIGH (100%) 1 minute; stir. If necessary, microwave an additional 15 seconds at a time, stirring after each heating, until chips are melted and mixture is smooth when stirred.

2. Refrigerate 3 hours or until firm. Shape mixture into 1-inch balls. Roll each ball in desired coatings. Cover; store in refrigerator.

Makes about 3 dozen truffles

GONE-TO-HEAVEN CHOCOLATE PIE

$^2/_3$ cup sugar

$^1/_3$ cup cornstarch

$^1/_2$ teaspoon salt

4 egg yolks

3 cups milk

2 tablespoons butter or margarine, softened

1 tablespoon vanilla extract

2 cups (12-ounce package) HERSHEY'S SPECIAL DARK® Chocolate Chips, divided

1 9-inch baked pie shell

Sweetened whipped cream or whipped topping (optional)

1. Stir together sugar, cornstarch and salt in 2-quart saucepan. Combine egg yolks and milk in bowl or container with pouring spout. Gradually blend milk mixture into sugar mixture.

2. Cook over medium heat, stirring constantly, until mixture comes to a boil. Boil and stir 1 minute. Remove from heat; stir in butter and vanilla. Add 1$^3/_4$ cups chocolate chips; stir until chips are melted and mixture is well blended. Pour into prepared pie shell; press plastic wrap onto filling. Cool. Refrigerate several hours or until chilled and firm. Remove plastic wrap and garnish with whipped cream and remaining chocolate chips, if desired. *Makes 6 to 8 servings*

CHOCOLATE BUTTERCREAM CHERRY CANDIES

About 48 maraschino cherries with stems, well drained
¼ cup (½ stick) butter, softened
2 cups powdered sugar
¼ cup HERSHEY'S Cocoa or HERSHEY'S SPECIAL DARK® Cocoa
1 to 2 tablespoons milk, divided
½ teaspoon vanilla extract
¼ teaspoon almond extract
White Chip Coating (recipe follows)
Chocolate Chip Drizzle (recipe follows)

1. Cover tray with wax paper. Lightly press cherries between layers of paper towels to remove excess moisture.

2. Beat butter, powdered sugar, cocoa and 1 tablespoon milk in small bowl until well blended; stir in vanilla and almond extract. If necessary, add remaining milk, one teaspoon at a time, until mixture will hold together but is not wet.

3. Mold scant teaspoon mixture around each cherry, covering completely; place on prepared tray. Cover; refrigerate 3 hours or until firm.

4. Prepare White Chip Coating. Holding each cherry by stem, dip into coating. Place on tray; refrigerate until firm.

5. About 1 hour before serving, prepare Chocolate Chip Drizzle; with tines of fork drizzle randomly over candies. Refrigerate until drizzle is firm. Store in refrigerator.

Makes about 48 candies

WHITE CHIP COATING: Place 2 cups (12-ounce package) HERSHEY'S Premier White Chips in small microwave-safe bowl; drizzle with 2 tablespoons vegetable oil. Microwave at HIGH (100%) 1 minute; stir. If necessary, microwave at HIGH an additional 15 seconds at a time, stirring after each heating just until chips are melted and mixture is smooth. If mixture thickens while coating, microwave at HIGH 15 seconds; stir until smooth.

CHOCOLATE CHIP DRIZZLE: Place ¼ cup HERSHEY'S Semi-Sweet Chocolate Chips and ¼ teaspoon shortening (do not use butter, margarine, spread or oil) in another small microwave-safe bowl. Microwave at HIGH (100%) 30 seconds to 1 minute; stir until chips are melted and mixture is smooth.

CHOCOLATE BUTTERCREAM CHERRY CANDIES

FLUTED KISSES® CUPS WITH PEANUT BUTTER FILLING

72 HERSHEY'S KISSES® Brand Milk Chocolates, divided
1 cup REESE'S® Creamy Peanut Butter
1 cup powdered sugar
1 tablespoon butter or margarine, softened

1. Line small baking cups (1¾ inches in diameter) with small paper baking liners. Remove wrappers from chocolates.

2. Place 48 chocolates in small microwave-safe bowl. Microwave on HIGH (100%) 1 minute or until chocolate is melted and smooth when stirred. Using small soft-bristled brush, coat inside of paper cups with melted chocolate.

3. Refrigerate 20 minutes; reapply melted chocolate to any thin spots. Refrigerate until firm, preferably overnight. Gently peel paper from chocolate cups.

4. Beat peanut butter, powdered sugar and butter with electric mixer on medium speed in small bowl until smooth. Spoon into chocolate cups. Before serving, top each cup with a chocolate piece. Cover; store cups in refrigerator. *Makes about 2 dozen pieces*

TIP

The chocolate cups can be prepared in advance. When firm, place cups in an air tight container and freeze until ready to use.

FLUTED KISSES® CUPS WITH PEANUT BUTTER FILLING

CREAMY CHOCOLATE AND PEACH LAYERED PUDDING

$\frac{1}{3}$ cup sugar
$\frac{1}{4}$ cup HERSHEY'S Cocoa
3 tablespoons cornstarch
$2\frac{2}{3}$ cups lowfat 2% milk
1 teaspoon vanilla extract
Peach Sauce (recipe follows)
$\frac{1}{3}$ cup frozen light non-dairy whipped topping, thawed

1. Stir together sugar, cocoa and cornstarch in medium saucepan; gradually stir in milk. Cook over medium heat, stirring constantly, until mixture comes to a boil; boil 1 minute. Remove from heat; stir in vanilla. Press plastic wrap directly onto surface. Cool completely.

2. Meanwhile, prepare Peach Sauce.

3. Layer chocolate mixture and Peach Sauce in 6 individual dessert dishes. Cover; refrigerate until cold. Serve with dollop of whipped topping. Garnish as desired.

Makes 6 servings

PEACH SAUCE: Place $1\frac{1}{2}$ cups fresh peach slices and 1 tablespoon sugar in blender container. Cover; blend until smooth. Stir together $\frac{1}{4}$ cup water and $1\frac{1}{2}$ teaspoons cornstarch in medium microwave-safe bowl until smooth. Add peach mixture; stir. Microwave at HIGH (100%) $2\frac{1}{2}$ to 3 minutes or until mixture boils, stirring after each minute. Cool completely. Makes about $1\frac{1}{3}$ cups sauce.

CREAMY CHOCOLATE AND PEACH LAYERED PUDDING

CHOCOLATE KISSES® MOUSSE

36 HERSHEY'S KISSES® Brand Milk Chocolates
1½ cups miniature marshmallows or 15 regular marshmallows
⅓ cup milk
2 teaspoons kirsch (cherry brandy) or ¼ teaspoon almond extract
6 to 8 drops red food color (optional)
1 cup cold whipping cream
Additional HERSHEY'S KISSES® Brand Milk chocolates (optional)

1. Remove wrappers from chocolates. Combine marshmallows and milk in small saucepan. Cook over low heat, stirring constantly, until marshmallows are melted and mixture is smooth. Remove from heat.

2. Pour ⅓ cup marshmallow mixture into medium bowl; stir in kirsch and food color, if desired. Set aside. To remaining marshmallow mixture, add 36 chocolates; return to low heat, stirring constantly until chocolate is melted. Remove from heat; cool to room temperature.

3. Beat whipping cream in small bowl until stiff. Fold 1 cup whipped cream into chocolate mixture. Gradually fold remaining whipped cream into reserved marshmallow mixture. Fill 4 parfait glasses about ¾ full with chocolate mousse; spoon or pipe reserved marshmallow mixture on top. Refrigerate 3 to 4 hours or until set. Garnish with additional chocolates, if desired. *Males 4 servings*

NO-BAKE CHERRY CHOCOLATE SHORTCAKE

  1 frozen loaf pound cake (10¾ ounces), thawed
  1 can (21 ounces) cherry pie filling, chilled
  ⅓ cup HERSHEY'S Cocoa or HERSHEY'S SPECIAL DARK® Cocoa
  ½ cup powdered sugar
  1 tub (8 ounces) frozen non-dairy whipped topping, thawed (3 cups)

1. Slice pound cake horizontally into three layers. Place bottom cake layer on serving plate; top with half the pie filling, using mostly cherries. Repeat with middle cake layer and remaining pie filling; place rounded layer on top. Cover; refrigerate several hours.

2. Sift cocoa and powdered sugar onto whipped topping; stir until mixture is blended and smooth. Immediately spread over top and sides of cake, covering completely. Refrigerate leftover shortcake. *Makes about 6 servings*

TIP

This chocolately recipe is a delicious twist on traditional shortcake.

EASY CHOCOLATE CHEESE PIE

2 bars (1 ounce *each*) HERSHEY'S Unsweetened Baking Chocolate, broken into pieces
$\frac{1}{4}$ cup ($\frac{1}{2}$ stick) butter or margarine, softened
$\frac{3}{4}$ cup sugar
1 package (3 ounces) cream cheese, softened
1 teaspoon milk
2 cups frozen whipped topping, thawed
1 packaged crumb crust (6 ounces)
Additional whipped topping (optional)

1. Place chocolate in small microwave-safe bowl. Microwave at HIGH (100%) 1 to $1\frac{1}{2}$ minutes or until chocolate is melted and smooth when stirred.

2. Beat butter, sugar, cream cheese and milk in medium bowl until well blended and smooth; fold in melted chocolate.

3. Fold in 2 cups whipped topping; spoon into crust. Cover; refrigerate until firm, about 3 hours. Garnish with additional whipped topping, if desired. *Makes 6 to 8 servings*

TIP

Chocolate curls are a beautiful finishing touch for the top of a delicious dessert. Place $\frac{1}{4}$ cup chocolate chips on a small microwavable plate and heat at HIGH 5 to 10 seconds. (Chocolate should still be firm.) Pull a vegetable peeler across the chocolate to create curls. Place the curls on a waxed paper-lined baking sheet and refrigerate 15 minutes or until firm.

EASY CHOCOLATE CHEESE PIE

SPECIAL DARK® FUDGE FONDUE

2 cups (12-ounce package) HERSHEY'S SPECIAL DARK® Chocolate Chips
½ cup light cream
2 teaspoons vanilla extract
   Assorted fondue dippers such as marshmallows, cherries, grapes,
      mandarin orange segments, pineapple chunks, strawberries, slices
      of other fresh fruits, small pieces of cake, or small brownies

1. Place chocolate chips and light cream in medium microwave-safe bowl. Microwave on HIGH (100%) 1 minute or just until chips are melted and mixture is smooth when stirred. Stir in vanilla.

2. Pour into fondue pot or chafing dish; serve warm with fondue dippers. If mixture thickens, stir in additional light cream, one tablespoon at a time. Refrigerate leftover fondue.

STOVETOP DIRECTIONS
Combine chocolate chips and light cream in heavy medium saucepan. Cook over low heat, stirring constantly, until chips are melted and mixture is hot. Stir in vanilla, and continue as in Step 2 above. *Makes 1½ cups fondue*

SPECIAL DARK® FUDGE FONDUE

EASY PEANUT BUTTER CHIP PIE

1 package (3 ounces) cream cheese, softened
1 teaspoon lemon juice
1⅔ cups (10-ounce package) REESE'S® Peanut Butter Chips, divided
⅔ cup sweetened condensed milk (not evaporated milk)
1 cup (½ pint) cold whipping cream, divided
1 packaged chocolate or graham cracker crumb crust (6 ounces)
1 tablespoon powdered sugar
1 teaspoon vanilla extract

1. Beat cream cheese and lemon juice in medium bowl until fluffy, about 2 minutes; set aside.

2. Place 1 cup peanut butter chips and sweetened condensed milk in medium microwave-safe bowl. Microwave at HIGH (100%) 45 seconds; stir. If necessary, microwave an additional 15 seconds at a time, stirring after each heating, until chips are melted and mixture is smooth when stirred.

3. Add warm peanut butter mixture to cream cheese mixture. Beat on medium speed until blended, about 1 minute. Beat ½ cup whipping cream in small bowl until stiff; fold into peanut butter mixture. Pour into crust. Cover; refrigerate several hours or overnight until firm.

4. Just before serving, combine remaining ½ cup whipping cream, powdered sugar and vanilla in small bowl. Beat until stiff; spread over filling. Garnish with remaining peanut butter chips. Cover; refrigerate leftover pie. *Makes 6 to 8 servings*

EASY PEANUT BUTTER CHIP PIE

TWO-TONE CREAM PIE

1 package (6-serving size) vanilla cook & serve pudding and pie filling mix*
3½ cups milk
1 cup REESE'S® Peanut Butter Chips
1 cup HERSHEY'S Semi-Sweet Chocolate Chips or HERSHEY'S MINI CHIPS™ Semi-Sweet Chocolate Chips
1 baked (9-inch) pie crust, cooled

*Do not use instant pudding mix.

1. Combine pudding mix and milk in medium saucepan. Cook over medium heat, stirring constantly, until mixture comes to full boil; remove from heat. Pour 2 cups hot pudding into small bowl and add peanut butter chips; stir until chips are melted and mixture is smooth.

2. Add chocolate chips to remaining hot pudding; stir until chips are melted and mixture is smooth. Pour chocolate mixture into baked pie crust. Gently pour and spread peanut butter mixture over top. Press plastic wrap directly onto surface. Chill several hours or overnight. Garnish as desired. Refrigerate leftovers.

Makes 1 (9-inch) pie

CHOCOLATE-ORANGE ICE

2 cups water
⅔ cup sugar
2 tablespoons HERSHEY'S Cocoa
Strips of peel from 1 orange
½ cup fresh orange juice

1. Stir together water, sugar, cocoa and orange peel in medium saucepan. Cook over medium heat, stirring constantly, until mixture comes to a boil. Reduce heat; simmer 5 minutes, without stirring. Strain to remove orange peel; discard. Cover; refrigerate mixture several hours until cold.

2. Stir orange juice into chocolate mixture. Pour into 1-quart ice cream freezer container. Freeze according to manufacturer's directions.

Makes 6 servings

CHOCOLATE COCONUT BALLS

3 bars (1 ounce *each*) HERSHEY'S Unsweetened Baking Chocolate

¼ cup (½ stick) butter

½ cup sweetened condensed milk (not evaporated milk)

¾ cup granulated sugar

¼ cup water

1 tablespoon light corn syrup

1 teaspoon vanilla extract

2 cups MOUNDS® Sweetened Coconut Flakes

1 cup chopped nuts

Powdered sugar

1. Melt chocolate and butter in large heavy saucepan over very low heat. Add sweetened condensed milk; stir to blend. Remove from heat.

2. Stir together granulated sugar, water and corn syrup in small saucepan. Cook over medium heat, stirring constantly, until sugar is dissolved. Cook, without stirring, until mixture reaches 250°F on candy thermometer or until a small amount of syrup, when dropped into very cold water, forms a firm ball which does not flatten when removed from water. (Bulb of candy thermometer should not rest on bottom of saucepan.) Remove from heat; stir into chocolate mixture. Add vanilla, coconut and nuts; stir until well blended.

3. Refrigerate about 1 hour or until firm enough to handle. Shape into 1-inch balls; roll in powdered sugar. Store tightly covered in cool, dry place.

Makes about 4 dozen candies

NOTE: For best results, do not double this recipe.

Prep Time: 25 minutes
Cook Time: 20 minutes
Chill Time: 30 minutes

MILK CHOCOLATE POTS DE CRÈME

2 cups (11½-ounce package) HERSHEY'S Milk Chocolate Chips
½ cup light cream
½ teaspoon vanilla extract
   Sweetened whipped cream (optional)

1. Place chocolate chips and cream in medium microwave-safe bowl. Microwave on HIGH (100%) 1 minute or just until chips are melted and mixture is smooth when stirred. Stir in vanilla.

2. Pour into demitasse cups or very small dessert dishes. Cover; refrigerate until firm. Serve cold with sweetened whipped cream, if desired. *Makes 6 to 8 servings*

TIP

For a richer chocolate flavor, substitute HERSHEY'S Semi-Sweet Chocolate Chips for HERSHEY'S Milk Chocolate Chips.

MILK CHOCOLATE POTS DE CRÈME

HERSHEY'S COCOA CREAM PIE

1 unbaked 9-inch pie crust or graham cracker crumb crust
1¼ cups sugar
½ cup HERSHEY'S Cocoa
⅓ cup cornstarch
¼ teaspoon salt
3 cups milk
3 tablespoons butter or margarine
1½ teaspoons vanilla extract
Sweetened whipped cream

1. Prepare crust; cool.

2. Stir together sugar, cocoa, cornstarch and salt in medium saucepan. Gradually add milk, stirring until smooth. Cook over medium heat, stirring constantly, until mixture comes to a boil; boil 1 minute.

3. Remove from heat; stir in butter and vanilla. Pour into prepared crust. Press plastic wrap directly onto surface. Cool to room temperature. Refrigerate 6 to 8 hours. Serve with sweetened whipped cream. Garnish as desired. Cover; refrigerate leftover pie.

Makes 6 to 8 servings

HERSHEY'S COCOA CREAM PIE

EASY MINI KISSES®
CHOCO-CHERRY PIE

1 unbaked (9-inch) pie crust

1¾ cups (10-ounce package) HERSHEY'S MINI KISSES® Brand Milk Chocolates, divided

1½ cups miniature marshmallows

⅓ cup milk

1 cup (½ pint) cold whipping cream

1 can (21 ounces) cherry pie filling, chilled

Whipped topping

1. Prepare crust; cool.

2. Place 1 cup chocolate pieces, marshmallows and milk in medium microwave-safe bowl. Microwave at HIGH (100%) 1½ to 2 minutes or until chocolate is softened and mixture is melted and smooth when stirred; cool completely.

3. Beat whipping cream in small bowl until stiff; fold into chocolate mixture. Spoon into prepared crust. Cover; refrigerate 4 hours or until firm.

4. Garnish top of pie with cherry pie filling, whipped topping and remaining chocolates just before serving. Refrigerate leftover pie.   *Makes about 8 servings*

EASY MINI KISSES® CHOCO-CHERRY PIE

SWEETHEART CHOCOLATE MOUSSE

1 envelope unflavored gelatin
2 tablespoons cold water
¼ cup boiling water
1 cup sugar
½ cup HERSHEY'S Cocoa
2 cups (1 pint) cold whipping cream
2 teaspoons vanilla extract
Fresh raspberries or sliced strawberries

1. Sprinkle gelatin over cold water in small bowl; let stand 2 minutes to soften. Add boiling water; stir until gelatin is completely dissolved and mixture is clear. Cool slightly.

2. Mix sugar and cocoa in large bowl; add whipping cream and vanilla. Beat on medium speed, scraping bottom of bowl occasionally, until mixture is stiff. Pour in gelatin mixture; beat until well blended.

3. Spoon into dessert dishes. Refrigerate at least 30 minutes before serving. Garnish with fruit.

Makes about 8 servings

SWEETHEART CHOCOLATE MOUSSE

REFRESHING COCOA-FRUIT SHERBET

1 ripe medium banana
1½ cups orange juice
1 cup (½ pint) half-and-half
½ cup sugar
¼ cup HERSHEY'S Cocoa

1. Slice banana into blender container. Add orange juice; cover and blend until smooth. Add remaining ingredients; cover and blend well. Pour into 8- or 9-inch square pan. Cover; freeze until hard around edges.

2. Spoon partially frozen mixture into blender container. Cover; blend until smooth but not melted. Pour into 1-quart mold. Cover; freeze until firm. Unmold onto cold plate and slice. Garnish as desired. *Makes 8 servings*

VARIATION: Add 2 teaspoons orange-flavored liqueur with orange juice.

REFRESHING COCOA-FRUIT SHERBET

TIDAL WAVE COCOA ALMOND MOUSSE

⅔ cup sugar

⅓ cup HERSHEY'S Cocoa

1 envelope unflavored gelatin

1½ cups (12-ounce can) evaporated nonfat milk

½ teaspoon almond extract

1 envelope (1.3 ounces) dry whipped topping mix

½ cup cold nonfat milk

½ teaspoon vanilla extract

1. Stir together sugar, cocoa and gelatin in medium saucepan; stir in evaporated milk until blended. Let stand 1 minute to soften gelatin. Cook over low heat, stirring constantly, until gelatin is completely dissolved, about 5 minutes.

2. Remove from heat; pour mixture into large bowl. Stir in almond extract. Refrigerate, stirring occasionally, until mixture mounds slightly when dropped from spoon.

3. Prepare topping mix as directed on package, using ½ cup milk and ½ teaspoon vanilla. Reserve ½ cup topping for garnish (cover and refrigerate until ready to use); fold remaining topping into chocolate mixture. Let stand a few minutes; spoon into 7 individual dessert dishes. Cover; refrigerate until firm. Garnish with reserved topping. *Makes 7 servings*

TIDAL WAVE COCOA ALMOND MOUSSE

CHOCOLATE-BANANA SHERBET

2 ripe medium bananas
1 cup apricot nectar or peach or pineapple juice, divided
½ cup HERSHEY'S Semi-Sweet Chocolate Chips
2 tablespoons sugar
1 cup lowfat 2% milk

1. Slice bananas into blender container or food processor. Add ¾ cup fruit juice. Cover; blend until smooth.

2. Place chocolate chips, remaining ¼ cup fruit juice and sugar in small microwave-safe bowl. Microwave at HIGH (100%) 30 seconds; stir. If necessary, microwave at HIGH an additional 15 seconds at a time, stirring after each heating, just until chips are melted and mixture is smooth when stirred. Add to mixture in blender. Cover; blend until thoroughly combined. Add milk. Cover; blend until smooth. Pour into 8- or 9-inch square pan. Cover; freeze until hard around edges, about 2 hours.

3. Spoon partially frozen mixture in bowl or food processor; beat until smooth but not melted. Return mixture to pan. Cover; freeze until firm, stirring several times before mixture freezes.

4. Before serving, let stand at room temperature 10 to 15 minutes until slightly softened. Scoop into 8 individual dessert dishes.

Makes 8 servings

CHOCOLATE-BANANA SHERBET

WHITE & CHOCOLATE COVERED STRAWBERRIES

2 cups (12-ounce package) HERSHEY'S Premier White Chips
2 tablespoons shortening (do *not* use butter, margarine, spread or oil)
1 cup HERSHEY'S Semi-Sweet Chocolate Chips
4 cups (2 pints) fresh strawberries, rinsed, patted dry and chilled

1. Cover tray with wax paper.

2. Place white chips and 1 tablespoon shortening in medium microwave-safe bowl. Microwave at HIGH (100%) 1 minute; stir until chips are melted and mixture is smooth. If necessary, microwave at HIGH an additional 30 seconds at a time, just until smooth when stirred.

3. Holding by top, dip $2/3$ of each strawberry into white chip mixture; shake gently to remove excess. Place on prepare tray; refrigerate until coating is firm, at least 30 minutes.

4. Repeat microwave procedure with chocolate chips and remaining 1 tablespoon shortening in clean microwave-safe bowl. Dip lower $1/3$ of each berry into chocolate mixture. Refrigerate until firm. Cover; refrigerate leftover strawberries.

Makes 2 to 3 dozen berries

MOCHA TRUFFLES

$1/4$ cup whipping cream
3 tablespoons sugar
3 tablespoons butter
$1\frac{1}{2}$ teaspoons powdered instant coffee
$1/2$ cup HERSHEY'S Semi-Sweet Chocolate Chips
$1/2$ teaspoon vanilla extract
   Chopped nuts or HERSHEY'S Semi-Sweet Baking Chocolate, grated

1. Combine whipping cream, sugar, butter, and instant coffee in small saucepan. Cook over low heat, stirring constantly, just until mixture boils.

2.Remove from heat; immediately add chocolate chips. Stir until chips are melted and mixture is smooth when stirred; add vanilla. Pour into small bowl; refrigerate, stirring occasionally, until mixture begins to set. Cover; refrigerate several hours or overnight to allow mixture to ripen and harden.

3. Shape small amounts of mixture into 1-inch balls, working quickly to prevent melting; roll in nuts or chocolate. Cover, store in refrigerator. Serve cold.

Makes about 16 truffles

WHITE & CHOCOLATE COVERED STRAWBERRIES AND MOCHA TRUFFLES

TROPICAL CHOCOLATE ORANGE ICE MILK

$^2/_3$ cup nonfat dry milk powder

$^2/_3$ cup sugar

$^1/_4$ cup HERSHEY'S Cocoa

2 tablespoons cornstarch

4 cups (1 quart) nonfat milk, divided

$^1/_4$ teaspoon freshly grated orange peel

$^1/_8$ teaspoon orange extract

Orange Cups (optional, directions follow)

Additional freshly grated orange peel (optional)

1. Stir together milk powder, sugar, cocoa and cornstarch in medium saucepan. Gradually stir in 2 cups milk. Cook over medium heat, stirring constantly, until mixture is smooth and slightly thickened, about 5 minutes.

2. Remove from heat. Stir in remaining 2 cups milk, $^1/_4$ teaspoon orange peel and orange extract. Cover; refrigerate several hours until cold.

3. Pour mixture into 2-quart ice cream freezer container. Freeze according to manufacturer's directions. Before serving, let stand at room temperature until slightly softened. Make Orange Cups, if desired. Scoop $^1/_2$ cup ice milk into each cup or into 8 individual dessert dishes. Garnish with additional orange peel, if desired.

Makes 8 servings

ORANGE CUPS: Cut about 1-inch slice from tops of 8 oranges; discard. Using sharp knife, cut out and remove small triangle shaped notches around tops of oranges to make zig-zag pattern. Scoop out pulp; reserve for other uses.

TROPICAL CHOCOLATE ORANGE ICE MILK

COCOA BLACK FOREST CRÊPES

3 eggs
³⁄₄ cup water
¹⁄₂ cup light cream or half-and-half
³⁄₄ cup plus 2 tablespoons all-purpose flour
3 tablespoons HERSHEY'S Cocoa
2 tablespoons sugar
¹⁄₈ teaspoon salt
3 tablespoons butter or margarine, melted and cooled
    Cherry pie filling
    Chocolate Sauce (recipe follows)
    Sweetened whipped cream (optional)

1. Combine eggs, water and light cream in blender or food processor; blend 10 seconds. Add flour, cocoa, sugar, salt and butter; blend until smooth. Let stand at room temperature 30 minutes.

2. Spray 6-inch crêpe pan lightly with vegetable cooking spray; heat over medium heat. For each crêpe, pour 2 to 3 tablespoons batter into pan; lift and tilt pan to spread batter. Return to heat; cook until surface begins to dry. Loosen crêpe around edges; turn and lightly cook other side. Stack crêpes, placing wax paper between crêpes. Keep covered. (Refrigerate for later use, if desired.)

3. Just before serving, place 2 tablespoons pie filling onto each crêpe; roll up. Place crêpes on dessert plate. Prepare Chocolate Sauce; spoon over crêpes. Garnish with sweetened whipped cream, if desired. *Makes about 18 crêpes*

CHOCOLATE SAUCE: Stir together ³⁄₄ cup sugar and ¹⁄₃ cup HERSHEY'S Cocoa in small saucepan; add in ¹⁄₂ cup plus 2 tablespoons (5-ounce can) evaporated milk, ¹⁄₄ cup (¹⁄₂ stick) butter or margarine and ¹⁄₈ teaspoon salt. Cook over medium heat, stirring constantly, until mixture comes to a boil. Remove from heat; stir in 1 teaspoon kirsch (cherry brandy), if desired. Serve warm. Cover; refrigerate leftover sauce. Makes about 1¹⁄₂ cups sauce.

FUDGE-BOTTOMED CHOCOLATE LAYER PIE

1 cup HERSHEY'S SPECIAL DARK® Chocolate Chips, divided
2 tablespoons plus ¼ cup milk, divided
1 packaged chocolate crumb crust (6 ounces)
1½ cups miniature marshmallows
1 tub (8 ounces) frozen nondairy whipped topping, thawed and divided
Additional sweetened whipped cream or whipped topping (optional)

1. Place ⅓ cup chocolate chips and 2 tablespoons milk in microwave-safe bowl. Microwave 30 seconds at HIGH (100%); stir. If necessary, microwave an additional 15 seconds at a time, stirring after each heating, until chips are melted and mixture is smooth when stirred. Spread on bottom of crust. Refrigerate while preparing next step.

2. Place marshmallows, remaining ⅔ cup chocolate chips and remaining ¼ cup milk in small saucepan. Cook over medium heat, stirring constantly, until marshmallows are melted and mixture is well blended. Transfer to separate large bowl; cool completely.

3. Stir 2 cups whipped topping into cooled chocolate mixture; spread 2 cups mixture over chocolate in crust. Blend remaining whipped topping and remaining chocolate mixture; spread over surface of pie.

4. Cover; freeze several hours or until firm. Garnish as desired. Cover and freeze leftover pie.

Makes 6 to 8 servings

BREADS & MUFFINS

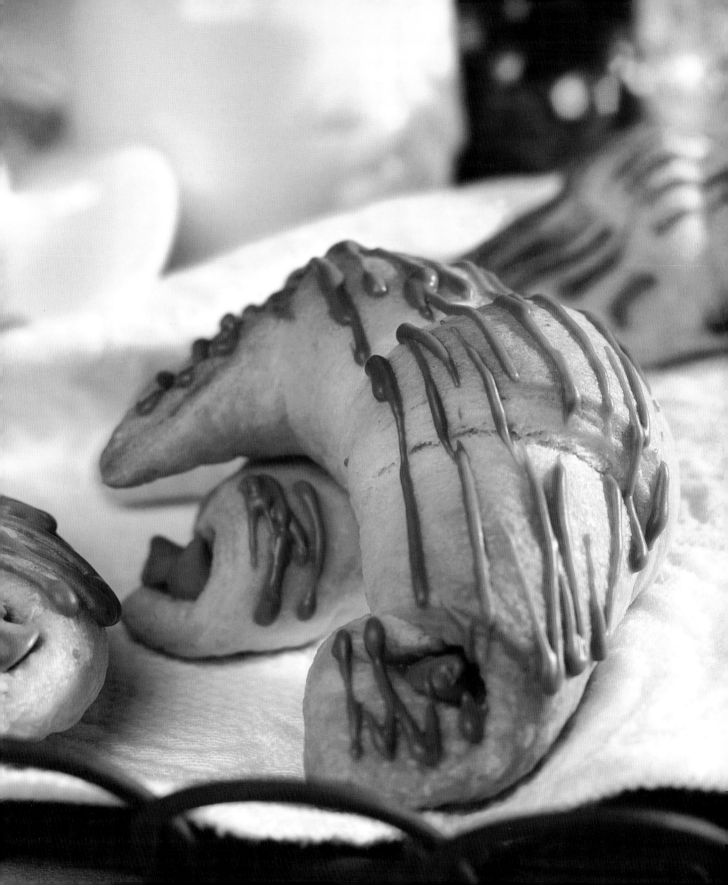

ORANGE STREUSEL COFFEECAKE

Cocoa Streusel (recipe follows)
¾ cup (1½ sticks) butter or margarine, softened
1 cup sugar
3 eggs
1 teaspoon vanilla extract
½ cup dairy sour cream
3 cups all-purpose flour
2 teaspoons baking powder
1 teaspoon baking soda
1 cup orange juice
2 teaspoons grated orange peel
½ cup orange marmalade or apple jelly

1. Prepare Cocoa Streusel. Heat oven to 350°F. Generously grease 12-cup fluted tube pan.

2. Beat butter and sugar in large bowl until well blended. Add eggs and vanilla; beat well. Add sour cream; beat until blended. Stir together flour, baking powder and baking soda; add alternately with orange juice to butter mixture, beating until well blended. Stir in orange peel.

3. Spread marmalade in bottom of prepared pan; sprinkle half of streusel over marmalade. Pour half of batter into pan, spreading evenly. Sprinkle remaining streusel over batter; spread remaining batter evenly over streusel.

4. Bake about 1 hour or until wooden pick inserted near center of cake comes out clean. Loosen cake from side of pan with metal spatula; immediately invert onto serving plate. Serve warm or cool. *Makes 12 servings*

COCOA STREUSEL: Stir together ⅔ cup packed light brown sugar, ½ cup chopped walnuts, ¼ cup HERSHEY'S Cocoa and ½ cup MOUNDS® Sweetened Coconut Flakes, if desired.

ORANGE STREUSEL COFFEECAKE

FUDGEY PEANUT BUTTER CHIP MUFFINS

$\frac{1}{2}$ cup applesauce

$\frac{1}{2}$ cup quick-cooking rolled oats

$\frac{1}{4}$ cup ($\frac{1}{2}$ stick) butter or margarine, softened

$\frac{1}{2}$ cup granulated sugar

$\frac{1}{2}$ cup packed light brown sugar

1 egg

$\frac{1}{2}$ teaspoon vanilla extract

$\frac{3}{4}$ cup all-purpose flour

$\frac{1}{4}$ cup HERSHEY'S SPECIAL DARK® Cocoa or HERSHEY'S Cocoa

$\frac{1}{2}$ teaspoon baking soda

$\frac{1}{4}$ teaspoon ground cinnamon (optional)

1 cup REESE'S® Peanut Butter Chips

Powdered sugar (optional)

1. Heat oven to 350°F. Line muffin cups ($2\frac{1}{2}$ inches in diameter) with paper bake cups.

2. Stir together applesauce and oats in small bowl; set aside. Beat butter, granulated sugar, brown sugar, egg and vanilla in large bowl until well blended. Add applesauce mixture; blend well. Stir together flour, cocoa, baking soda and cinnamon, if desired. Add to butter mixture, blending well. Stir in peanut butter chips. Fill muffin cups $\frac{3}{4}$ full with batter.

3. Bake 22 to 26 minutes or until wooden pick inserted in center comes out almost clean. Cool slightly in pan on wire rack. Sprinkle muffin tops with powdered sugar, if desired. Serve warm. *Makes 12 to 15 muffins*

FUDGEY CHOCOLATE CHIP MUFFINS: Omit Peanut Butter Chips. Add 1 cup HERSHEY'S Semi-Sweet Chocolate Chips.

FUDGEY PEANUT BUTTER CHIP MUFFINS

COCOA CHERRY-NUT SNACKING BREAD

$\frac{1}{2}$ cup (1 stick) butter or margarine, softened
1 cup sugar
2 eggs
1 cup buttermilk or sour milk*
1$\frac{3}{4}$ cups all-purpose flour
$\frac{1}{2}$ cup HERSHEY'S Cocoa
$\frac{1}{2}$ teaspoon baking powder
$\frac{1}{2}$ teaspoon baking soda
$\frac{1}{4}$ teaspoon salt
$\frac{1}{2}$ cup finely chopped walnuts
$\frac{1}{2}$ cup finely chopped maraschino cherries, drained
   Easy Vanilla Glaze (recipe follows)
   Maraschino cherries, halved (optional)
   Walnut halves (optional)

*To sour milk: Use 1 tablespoon white vinegar plus milk to equal 1 cup.

1. Heat oven to 350°F. Grease bottom only of 9×5×3-inch loaf pan.

2. Beat butter, sugar and eggs in large bowl until well blended. Blend in buttermilk. Stir together flour, cocoa, baking powder, baking soda and salt; gradually add to butter mixture, beating well. Stir in chopped walnuts and chopped cherries. Pour batter into prepared pan.

3. Bake 55 to 60 minutes or until wooden pick inserted in center comes out clean. (Bread will crack slightly in center.) Cool 15 minutes. Remove from pan to wire rack. Cool completely.

4. Prepare Easy Vanilla Glaze; drizzle over bread. Garnish with cherry halves and walnut halves, if desired. *Makes about 12 servings*

EASY VANILLA GLAZE

1 tablespoon butter or margarine
$\frac{1}{2}$ cup powdered sugar
2 teaspoons hot water

Place butter in small microwave-safe bowl. Microwave at HIGH (100%) 30 seconds or until melted. Add powdered sugar. Gradually add water; stir until smooth and of desired consistency. Add additional water, $\frac{1}{2}$ teaspoon at a time, if needed. Makes about $\frac{1}{4}$ cup glaze.

PEANUT BUTTER CHIP & BANANA MINI MUFFINS

        2 cups all-purpose biscuit baking mix
$\frac{1}{4}$ cup sugar
        2 tablespoons butter or margarine, softened
        1 egg
        1 cup mashed very ripe bananas (2 to 3 medium)
        1 cup REESE'S® Peanut Butter Chips
        Quick Glaze (recipe follows, optional)

1. Heat oven to 400°F. Grease small muffin cups ($1\frac{3}{4}$ inches in diameter).

2. Stir together baking mix, sugar, butter and egg in medium bowl; with fork, beat vigorously for 30 seconds. Stir in bananas and peanut butter chips. Fill muffin cups $\frac{2}{3}$ full with batter.

3. Bake 12 to 15 minutes or until golden brown. Meanwhile, prepare Quick Glaze, if desired. Immediately remove muffins from pan; dip tops of warm muffins into glaze. Serve warm.   *Makes about 4 dozen small muffins*

QUICK GLAZE

        $1\frac{1}{2}$ cups powdered sugar
        2 tablespoons water

Stir together powdered sugar and water in small bowl until smooth and of desired consistency. Add additional water, $\frac{1}{2}$ teaspoon at a time, if needed. Makes about $\frac{3}{4}$ cup glaze.

TIP

Don't stir muffin batter too much--overmixing will make the muffins tough. There should still be lumps in the batter; these will disappear during baking.

CHOCOLATE QUICKIE STICKIES

8 tablespoons (1 stick) butter or margarine, divided
¾ cup packed light brown sugar
4 tablespoons HERSHEY'S Cocoa, divided
5 teaspoons water
1 teaspoon vanilla extract
½ cup coarsely chopped nuts (optional)
2 cans (8 ounces each) refrigerated quick crescent dinner rolls
2 tablespoons granulated sugar

1. Heat oven to 350°F.

2. Melt 6 tablespoons butter in small saucepan over low heat; add brown sugar, 3 tablespoons cocoa and water. Cook over medium heat, stirring constantly, just until mixture comes to boil. Remove from heat; stir in vanilla. Spoon about 1 teaspoon chocolate mixture into each of 48 small muffin cups (1¾ inches in diameter). Sprinkle ½ teaspoon nuts, if desired, into each cup; set aside.

3. Unroll dough; separate into 8 rectangles; firmly press perforations to seal. Melt remaining 2 tablespoons butter; brush over rectangles. Stir together granulated sugar and remaining 1 tablespoon cocoa; sprinkle over rectangles. Starting at longer side, roll up each rectangle; pinch seams to seal. Cut each roll into 6 equal pieces. Press gently into prepared pans, cut-side down.

4. Bake 11 to 13 minutes or until light brown. Remove from oven; let cool 30 seconds. Invert onto cookie sheet. Let stand 1 minute; remove pans. Serve warm or cool completely.   *Makes 4 dozen small rolls*

NOTE: Rolls can be baked in two 8-inch round baking pans. Heat oven to 350°F. Cook chocolate mixture as directed; spread half of mixture in each pan. Prepare rolls as directed; place 24 pieces, cut-side down, in each pan. Bake 20 to 22 minutes. Cool and remove pans as directed above.

CHOCOLATE QUICKIE STICKIES

STAR-OF-THE-EAST FRUIT BREAD

$\frac{1}{2}$ cup (1 stick) butter or margarine, softened
1 cup sugar
2 eggs
1 teaspoon vanilla extract
2 cups all-purpose flour
1 teaspoon baking soda
$\frac{1}{4}$ teaspoon salt
1 cup mashed ripe bananas (about 3 medium)
1 can (11 ounces) mandarin orange segments, well-drained
1 cup HERSHEY'S Semi-Sweet Chocolate Chips
$\frac{1}{2}$ cup chopped dates or Calimyrna figs
$\frac{1}{2}$ cup chopped maraschino cherries, well-drained
   Chocolate Drizzle (recipe follows)

1. Heat oven to 350°F. Grease two $8\frac{1}{2}\times4\frac{1}{2}\times2\frac{5}{8}$-inch loaf pans.

2. Beat butter and sugar in large bowl until fluffy. Add eggs and vanilla; beat well. Stir together flour, baking soda and salt; add alternately with mashed bananas to butter mixture, blending well. Stir in orange segments, chocolate chips, dates and cherries. Divide batter evenly between prepared pans.

3. Bake 40 to 50 minutes or until golden brown. Cool; remove from pans. Drizzle tops of loaves with Chocolate Drizzle. Store tightly wrapped.   *Makes 2 loaves*

CHOCOLATE DRIZZLE: Combine $\frac{1}{2}$ cup HERSHEY'S Semi-Sweet Chocolate Chips and 2 tablespoons whipping cream in small microwave-safe bowl. Microwave at HIGH (100%) 30 seconds; stir. If necessary, microwave at HIGH an additional 15 seconds; stir until chips are melted and mixture is smooth when stirred. Makes about $\frac{1}{2}$ cup.

STAR-OF-THE-EAST FRUIT BREAD

COCOA BRUNCH RINGS

$\frac{1}{2}$ cup milk
$\frac{1}{2}$ cup sugar
1 teaspoon salt
$\frac{1}{2}$ cup (1 stick) butter or margarine
2 packages active dry yeast
$\frac{1}{2}$ cup warm water
2 eggs, slightly beaten
$3\frac{1}{2}$ to $3\frac{3}{4}$ cups all-purpose flour
$\frac{3}{4}$ cup HERSHEY'S Cocoa
Orange Filling (recipe follows)

1. Scald milk in small saucepan over medium heat; stir in sugar, salt and butter. Cool to lukewarm.

2. Dissolve yeast in warm water (105° to 115°F) in large bowl; add milk mixture, eggs and 2 cups of the flour. Beat on medium speed of mixer 2 minutes until smooth. Stir together $1\frac{1}{2}$ cups of the flour and the cocoa; stir into yeast mixture.

3. Turn dough out onto well-floured board; knead in more flour until dough is smooth enough to handle. Knead about 5 minutes or until smooth and elastic. Place in greased bowl; turn dough to grease top. Cover; let rise in warm place until doubled, about 1 to $1\frac{1}{2}$ hours. Punch down dough; turn over. Cover; let rise 30 minutes longer. Prepare Orange Filling; set aside.

4. Heat oven to 350°F. Grease two 4- to 6-cup ring molds. Divide dough in half. On lightly floured board, roll out each half to a 13×9-inch rectangle. Spread one-fourth of Orange Filling on each rectangle to within $\frac{1}{2}$ inch of edges; reserve remaining filling for frosting. Roll up dough from long side as for jelly roll; pinch edge to seal. Cut rolls into 1-inch slices. Place slices, sealed edges down, in prepared ring molds. Tilt slices slightly, overlapping so filling shows. Cover; let rise in warm place until doubled, about 45 minutes.

5. Bake 20 to 25 minutes or until golden brown. Immediately remove from molds and place on serving plates. Frost with remaining Orange Filling or, if a glaze is preferred, stir in a few drops orange juice; spoon over rings. Serve warm. *Makes 2 rings*

ORANGE FILLING

3 cups powdered sugar
6 tablespoons butter or margarine, softened
$\frac{1}{4}$ cup orange juice
4 teaspoons grated orange peel

Combine powdered sugar, butter, orange juice and orange peel in small bowl; beat on low speed until smooth.

Makes about 2 cups filling

CHOCOLATE STREUSEL COFFEECAKE

Chocolate Streusel (recipe follows)
$\frac{1}{2}$ cup (1 stick) butter or margarine, softened
1 cup sugar
3 eggs
1 container (8 ounce) dairy sour cream
1 teaspoon vanilla extract
2 cups all-purpose flour
1 teaspoon baking powder
1 teaspoon baking soda
$\frac{1}{4}$ teaspoon salt

1. Heat oven to 350°F. Grease and flour 12-cup fluted tube pan. Prepare Chocolate Streusel; set aside.

2. Beat butter and sugar in large bowl until fluffy. Add eggs; blend well on low speed of mixer. Stir in sour cream and vanilla. Combine flour, baking powder, baking soda and salt in separate bowl; add to batter. Blend well.

3. Sprinkle 1 cup Chocolate Streusel into prepared pan. Spread one third of the batter (about $1\frac{1}{3}$ cups) in pan; sprinkle with half the remaining streusel (about 1 cup). Repeat layers, ending with batter on top.

4. Bake 50 to 55 minutes or until wooden pick inserted near center comes out clean. Cool 10 minutes; invert onto serving plate. Cool completely.

Makes 12 to 16 servings

CHOCOLATE STREUSEL

$\frac{3}{4}$ cup packed light brown sugar
$\frac{1}{4}$ cup all-purpose flour
$\frac{1}{4}$ cup ($\frac{1}{2}$ stick) butter or margarine, softened
$\frac{3}{4}$ cup chopped nuts
$\frac{3}{4}$ cup HERSHEY'S MINI CHIPS™ Semi-Sweet Chocolate Chips

Combine brown sugar, flour and butter in medium bowl until crumbly. Stir in nuts and small chocolate chips. Makes about $2\frac{1}{2}$ cups streusel.

REESE'S® PEANUT BUTTER AND MILK CHOCOLATE CHIP CRESCENTS

½ cup REESE'S® Peanut Butter and Milk Chocolate Chips
2 tablespoons finely chopped nuts
1 can (8 ounces) refrigerated quick crescent dinner rolls
Peanut Butter Chocolate Drizzle (recipe follows) or powdered sugar (optional)

1. Heat oven to 375°F.

2. Stir together chips and nuts in small bowl. Unroll dough to form 8 triangles. Lightly sprinkle 1 heaping tablespoon chip mixture on top of each; gently press into dough. Starting at shortest side of triangle, roll dough to opposite point. Place rolls, point side down, on ungreased cookie sheet; curve into crescent shape.

3. Bake 10 to 12 minutes or until golden brown. Prepare Peanut Butter Chocolate Drizzle; drizzle over crescents or sprinkle with powdered sugar, if desired. Serve warm.

Makes 8 crescents

PEANUT BUTTER CHOCOLATE DRIZZLE: Place ¼ cup REESE'S® Peanut Butter and Milk Chocolate Chips and 1 teaspoon shortening (do *not* use butter, margarine or oil) in small microwave-safe bowl. Microwave at HIGH (100%) 30 seconds; stir. If necessary, microwave at HIGH an additional 15 seconds at a time, stirring after each heating, just until chips are melted when stirred.

TIP

These crescents make a terrific sweet breakfast treat and an even better simple dessert.

REESE'S® PEANUT BUTTER AND MILK CHOCOLATE CHIP CRESCENTS

BERRY LOAF

2 cups all-purpose flour
1 cup sugar
1½ teaspoons baking powder
1 teaspoon salt
½ teaspoon baking soda
¾ cup orange juice
1 teaspoon freshly grated orange peel
2 tablespoons shortening
1 egg, slightly beaten
1 cup chopped fresh cranberries
1 cup HERSHEY'S MINI CHIPS™ Semi-Sweet Chocolate Chips
¾ cup chopped nuts
Powdered Sugar Glaze (recipe follows, optional)

1. Heat oven to 350°F. Grease 9×5×3-inch loaf pan.

2. Stir together flour, sugar, baking powder, salt and baking soda in large bowl. Add orange juice, orange peel, shortening and egg; stir until well blended. Stir in cranberries, small chocolate chips and nuts. Pour batter into prepared pan.

3. Bake 1 hour 5 minutes to 1 hour 10 minutes or until wooden pick inserted in center comes out clean. Cool 10 minutes; remove from pan to wire rack. Prepare Powdered Sugar Glaze, if desired; spread over top of loaf. Cool completely. Garnish as desired.

Makes 1 loaf (14 servings)

POWDERED SUGAR GLAZE

1 cup powdered sugar
1 tablespoon milk
1 teaspoon butter or margarine, softened
½ teaspoon vanilla extract

Stir together powdered sugar, milk, butter and vanilla in small bowl; beat until smooth and of desired consistency. Add additional milk, 1 teaspoon at a time, if needed. Makes about ½ cup glaze.

(LEFT TO RIGHT): COCOA CHERRY-NUT SNACKING BREAD (PAGE 230) AND BERRY LOAF

EASIER CHOCOLATE-FILLED BRAID

Chocolate Nut Filling (recipe follows)
2½ to 2¾ cups all-purpose flour, divided
2 tablespoons sugar
½ teaspoon salt
1 package rapid-rise yeast
½ cup milk
¼ cup water
½ cup (1 stick) butter or margarine
1 egg, at room temperature
Vegetable oil
Powdered Sugar Glaze (page 244, optional)

1. Heat oven to 375°F. Grease baking sheet. Prepare Chocolate Nut Filling.

2. Stir together 1½ cups flour, sugar, salt and yeast in large bowl of heavy duty mixer. Combine milk, water and butter in small saucepan; over low heat, heat just until very warm, 125° to 130°F. (Butter might not be melted.) Gradually add to dry ingredients; beat on medium speed of mixer 2 minutes. Add egg and 1 cup flour; beat 2 minutes. Stir in enough remaining flour to form stiff dough. Cover; let rest 10 minutes.

3. Onto well-floured board, turn out dough; roll into 18×10-inch rectangle. Transfer to prepared baking sheet. Spread Chocolate Nut Filling lengthwise down center third of dough. Cut 1-inch-wide strips diagonally on both sides of dough to within ¾ inch of filling. Alternately fold opposite strips of dough at angle across filling. Shape into ring; pinch ends together. Brush lightly with oil; let stand 10 minutes.

4. Bake 20 to 25 minutes or until lightly browned. Remove from baking sheet to wire rack. Cool completely. Prepare Powdered Sugar Glaze, if desired; drizzle over braid.

Makes 10 to 12 servings

CHOCOLATE NUT FILLING

¾ cup HERSHEY'S Semi-Sweet Chocolate Chips
2 tablespoons sugar
⅓ cup evaporated milk
½ cup chopped nuts
1 teaspoon vanilla extract
¼ teaspoon ground cinnamon

Stir together chocolate chips, sugar and evaporated milk in small saucepan. Over low heat, cook, stirring constantly, until chips are melted and mixture is smooth. Stir in nuts, vanilla and cinnamon. Cool completely. Makes about 2 cups.

continued on page 244

EASIER CHOCOLATE-FILLED BRAID

Easier Chocolate-Filled Braid, continued

POWDERED SUGAR GLAZE

1 cup powdered sugar
1 tablespoon milk
1 teaspoon butter or margarine, softened
½ teaspoon vanilla extract

Stir together powdered sugar, milk, butter and vanilla in small bowl; beat until smooth and of desired consistency. Add additional milk, 1 teaspoon at a time, if needed. Makes about ½ cup glaze.

CHIPPY BANANA BREAD

⅓ cup butter or margarine, softened
⅔ cup sugar
2 eggs
2 tablespoons milk
1¾ cups all-purpose flour
1¼ teaspoons baking powder
¾ teaspoon salt
½ teaspoon baking soda
1 cup mashed ripe bananas
1 cup HERSHEY'S Semi-Sweet Chocolate Chips or HERSHEY'S Cinnamon Chips

1. Heat oven to 350°F. Lightly grease 8×4×2-inch loaf pan.

2. Beat butter and sugar in large bowl on medium speed of mixer until creamy. Add eggs, one at a time, beating well after each addition. Add milk; beat until blended.

3. Stir together flour, baking powder, salt and baking soda; add alternately with bananas to butter mixture, beating until smooth after each addition. Gently fold in chocolate chips. Pour batter into prepared pan.

4. Bake 60 to 65 minutes or until wooden pick inserted near center comes out clean. Cool 10 minutes. Remove from pan to wire rack; cool completely. For easier slicing, wrap in foil and store overnight. *Makes 12 servings*

PEANUT BUTTER COFFEECAKE

1²⁄₃ cups (10-ounce package) REESE'S® Peanut Butter Chips

  2 tablespoons shortening (do *not* use butter, margarine, spread or oil)

2¹⁄₄ cups all-purpose flour

1¹⁄₂ cups packed light brown sugar

 ¹⁄₂ cup (1 stick) butter or margarine, softened

  1 teaspoon baking powder

¹⁄₂ teaspoon baking soda

  1 cup milk

  3 eggs

  1 teaspoon vanilla extract

  1 cup REESE'S® Peanut Butter Chips or HERSHEY'S MINI CHIPS Semi-Sweet Chocolate Chips

1. Heat oven to 350°F. Grease bottom of 13×9×2-inch baking pan.

2. Place 1²⁄₃ cups peanut butter chips and shortening in microwave-safe bowl. Microwave at HIGH (100%) 1 minute; stir. If necessary, microwave at HIGH an additional 15 seconds at a time, stirring after each heating, just until chips are melted when stirred.

3. Combine flour, brown sugar, butter and peanut butter chip mixture in large bowl. Beat on low speed of mixer until mixture resembles small crumbs; reserve 1 cup crumbs. To remaining crumb mixture, add baking powder, baking soda, milk, eggs and vanilla; beat until well combined. Pour batter into prepared pan; sprinkle with reserved crumbs.

4. Bake 35 to 40 minutes or until wooden pick inserted in center comes out clean. Remove from oven to wire rack; immediately sprinkle 1 cup peanut butter or small chocolate chips over top. Cool completely. *Makes 12 to 15 servings*

CINNAMON CHIP FILLED CRESCENTS

2 cans (8 ounces *each*) refrigerated quick crescent dinner rolls
2 tablespoons butter or margarine, melted
1⅔ cups (10-ounce package) HERSHEY'S Cinnamon Chips, divided
Cinnamon Chips Drizzle (recipe follows)

1. Heat oven to 375°F. Unroll dough; separate into 16 triangles.

2. Spread melted butter on each triangle. Sprinkle 1 cup cinnamon chips evenly over triangles; gently press chips into dough. Roll from shortest side of triangle to opposite point. Place, point side down, on ungreased cookie sheet; curve into crescent shape.

3. Bake 8 to 10 minutes or until golden brown. Drizzle with Cinnamon Chips Drizzle. Serve warm.

Makes 16 crescents

CINNAMON CHIPS DRIZZLE: Place remaining ⅔ cup chips and 1½ teaspoons shortening (do *not* use butter, margarine, spread or oil) in small microwave-safe bowl. Microwave at HIGH (100%) 1 minute; stir until chips are melted.

TIP

To reheat leftover crescents, place on microwave-safe plate. Microwave at HIGH (100%) 15 to 20 seconds or until warm.

CINNAMON CHIP FILLED CRESCENTS

ORANGE CHOCOLATE CHIP BREAD

$\frac{1}{2}$ cup nonfat milk

$\frac{1}{2}$ cup plain nonfat yogurt

$\frac{1}{3}$ cup sugar

$\frac{1}{4}$ cup orange juice

1 egg, slightly beaten

1 tablespoon freshly grated orange peel

3 cups all-purpose biscuit baking mix

$\frac{1}{2}$ cup HERSHEY'S MINI CHIPS™ Semi-Sweet Chocolate Chips

1. Heat oven to 350°F. Grease 9×5×3-inch loaf pan or spray with vegetable cooking spray.

2. Stir together milk, yogurt, sugar, orange juice, egg and orange peel in large bowl; add baking mix. With spoon, beat until well blended, about 1 minute. Stir in small chocolate chips. Pour into prepared pan.

3. Bake 45 to 50 minutes or until wooden pick inserted in center comes out clean. Cool 10 minutes; remove from pan to wire rack. Cool completely before slicing. Garnish as desired. Wrap leftover bread in foil or plastic wrap. Store at room temperature or freeze for longer storage.

Makes 1 loaf (16 slices)

ORANGE CHOCOLATE CHIP BREAD

METRIC CONVERSION CHART

VOLUME MEASUREMENTS (dry)

$^1/_8$ teaspoon = 0.5 mL
$^1/_4$ teaspoon = 1 mL
$^1/_2$ teaspoon = 2 mL
$^3/_4$ teaspoon = 4 mL
1 teaspoon = 5 mL
1 tablespoon = 15 mL
2 tablespoons = 30 mL
$^1/_4$ cup = 60 mL
$^1/_3$ cup = 75 mL
$^1/_2$ cup = 125 mL
$^2/_3$ cup = 150 mL
$^3/_4$ cup = 175 mL
1 cup = 250 mL
2 cups = 1 pint = 500 mL
3 cups = 750 mL
4 cups = 1 quart = 1 L

VOLUME MEASUREMENTS (fluid)

1 fluid ounce (2 tablespoons) = 30 mL
4 fluid ounces ($^1/_2$ cup) = 125 mL
8 fluid ounces (1 cup) = 250 mL
12 fluid ounces (1$^1/_2$ cups) = 375 mL
16 fluid ounces (2 cups) = 500 mL

WEIGHTS (mass)

$^1/_2$ ounce = 15 g
1 ounce = 30 g
3 ounces = 90 g
4 ounces = 120 g
8 ounces = 225 g
10 ounces = 285 g
12 ounces = 360 g
16 ounces = 1 pound = 450 g

DIMENSIONS

$^1/_{16}$ inch = 2 mm
$^1/_8$ inch = 3 mm
$^1/_4$ inch = 6 mm
$^1/_2$ inch = 1.5 cm
$^3/_4$ inch = 2 cm
1 inch = 2.5 cm

OVEN TEMPERATURES

250°F = 120°C
275°F = 140°C
300°F = 150°C
325°F = 160°C
350°F = 180°C
375°F = 190°C
400°F = 200°C
425°F = 220°C
450°F = 230°C

BAKING PAN SIZES

Utensil	Size in Inches/Quarts	Metric Volume	Size in Centimeters
Baking or Cake Pan (square or rectangular)	8 × 8 × 2	2 L	20 × 20 × 5
	9 × 9 × 2	2.5 L	23 × 23 × 5
	12 × 8 × 2	3 L	30 × 20 × 5
	13 × 9 × 2	3.5 L	33 × 23 × 5
Loaf Pan	8 × 4 × 3	1.5 L	20 × 10 × 7
	9 × 5 × 3	2 L	23 × 13 × 7
Round Layer Cake Pan	8 × 1½	1.2 L	20 × 4
	9 × 1½	1.5 L	23 × 4
Pie Plate	8 × 1¼	750 mL	20 × 3
	9 × 1¼	1 L	23 × 3
Baking Dish or Casserole	1 quart	1 L	—
	1½ quart	1.5 L	—
	2 quart	2 L	—